Practical Issues
of This Life

Practical Issues Of This Life

WATCHMAN NEE

Translated from the Chinese

Christian Fellowship Publishers, Inc.

New York

Available from the Publishers at:

Box 1021
Manassas, Virginia 22110

TRANSLATOR'S PREFACE

Life on earth has its many cares and problems. Yet not because we are Christians are we therefore exempt from having them. Nevertheless, God has given us His precious and exceedingly great promises that we may live a life of heaven on earth.

In the pages that are to follow, Watchman Nee takes up these various problems of this life, such problems as tears, the temper, our tongue, and so forth, and then shows us how they can be transformed by the grace of God and the power of the Holy Spirit into values of eternal worth. Instead of being smothered, we may breathe the air of heaven.

The selection of messages included in this volume, dealing as they all do with the practical issues of this life, were given by the author on various occasions during the earlier days of his ministry in China. The truths contained are nonetheless relevant and applicable to us today, since in spite of the great changes that have occurred in the world, this life itself retains all the cares and problems which it has always had. In this connection, we need again to be reminded of our Lord's admonition to His disciples: "Take heed to yourselves, lest haply your hearts be overcharged with . . . cares of this life, and that day come on you suddenly as a snare" (Luke 21.34).

CONTENTS

Precious Are the Tears

Who [Christ] in the days of his flesh, having offered up prayers and supplications with strong crying and tears unto him that was able to save him from death, and having been heard for his godly fear. (Heb. 5.7)

Today I would like for us to examine together one special matter that has been on my heart. It concerns something which everybody has, though it is not always evident. It is often something done by us, yet not done every time. And what is that? It is the shedding of tears. I wonder if you know the significance of tears? It is a good sign if a person is able to shed tears. An individual who had had much experience in spiritual matters once made this statement: Giving your love to a person who cannot shed tears is like handing over your money bag to a thief to keep. This is quite true. A person often feels uneasy about giving his love to one who cannot shed tears. For tears are the one thing that is indispensable in this world. It can rightly be said that a person who is unable to shed tears has lost something of the very essence of man: he can no longer be considered as being human.

I strongly repudiate any man who is so haughty as to condemn tears in men. He may think himself brave for not shedding tears. He may deem himself as nobler and superior to others. But facts just do not bear this out! Let me tell you, a dry eye reveals a dry and hard heart. Such a heart has become rebellious, void of feeling, insensitive as wood and stone. Oftentimes tears betray the true heart condition of a person. It may be said that nothing discloses the inward state of a human heart more than do tears. Let me say from conviction that tears are the outlet of the heart.

How is this so? Well, suppose I am exceedingly sad today; so sad, in fact, that I can neither sigh nor talk—nor can I eat, sleep, nor work. Now what would you think would be the best way to dispel my sadness? If you were to ask a doctor how to cure such depression, he might perhaps use psychology by suggesting that I should invite my most intimate friends over for a heart-to-heart talk, or that I should listen to a few jokes so as to laugh off my gloom, or that I should visit some beautiful scenic places, or that I should take a walk, or that I should listen to some music so as to soothe my heart and forget my sorrow. Let me tell you, none of these ideas will work. But should the doctor be one who is deep in life experience, he would declare to me instead: Have a good cry and you will find that everything will be all right. Is this not true? When pressure builds up within you to an unbearable degree, you will discover that just two drops of tears from your eyes will release all the tension and settle every problem. How strange that what is in the heart finds its exit through the eyes. It seems as though the eyes have become the outlet of the heart. For as the tears flow, the heart is opened up.

I recall that there was once a disabled person who suffered greatly because of his physical deficiency. Nothing seemed to please him, and so he began to harbor the thought of suicide. For seven long years such anguish had burned as fire within him. Then one day he attended a concert. All those present were enthralled by the excellent performance, and their souls were enraptured. But what about this one man? His conduct was quite different. He just shed two drops of tears. So that when people saw it they said to him: "Is not today's music most inspiring? Why then do you shed tears?" He answered them, "Formerly I was depressed and dejected, but as I listened to the music, my tears began to fall, and now I feel fine." Music therefore seemed to open a hole in this man's heart and caused his tears to flow. His heart originally had been filled with melancholy; but then his tears began to fall and the melancholy commenced to flow out with them. The humanity that had been so bound up and concealed by melancholia had at last been freed by tears. Now such an ability to shed tears demonstrates the humanity in a man. Some may regard tears as a sign of weakness; but quite the contrary, the one who has no tears to shed has buried his humanity.

Tears are the common portion which all mankind shares. And our Lord was no exception; He too shed tears. Though the Bible mentions the joy of the Lord, it never records His laughter. But it does recount the fact of His shedding tears. We notice in Hebrews 5.7 that the tears of the Lord are spoken of in plural number, perhaps indicating that He frequently shed tears. Isaiah 53 likewise indicates that Christ was "a man of sorrows, and acquainted with grief" (v.3).

It can truly be said that tears are most precious. Physically speaking, only a tear can wash a man's eyes. The world has so much dust and dirt constantly intruding upon them that, fortunately, with the incessant washing of tears a person may have clearer sight. Were there no tears in man's eyes, then most likely no one could see anything clearly.

Yet tears have this cleansing effect not only in the physical realm, they have the same effect in the spiritual realm. In the physical realm, a few more tears will cause you to see more clearly. Similarly, without a few tears your spiritual eyes would soon lose their function. Mr. D. H. Panton once told a young couple that everything was fine with them except for one point. If they would observe this one thing more they would be perfect. The point he had in mind was a desiring of the coming of the Lord. During that evening the husband said to his wife: "Let us heed the word of the old man this time. Let us pray carefully for this matter this evening." Whereupon he prayed faithfully concerning this matter, and expected his wife to continue in prayer as well. But she did not pray in this way, for, she thought to herself, Why *should* I ask the Lord to come quickly, since I have a good family, the relationship between my husband and me is most cordial, our living is quite comfortable, our house is very cozy, and everything seems to be going along exceedingly well? Seven months went by, and the husband suddenly passed away. Later, when the wife saw Mr. Panton, she took his hand and wept, saying, "Since the day of my husband's passing I have been asking daily for the soon return of the Lord." Tears had thus cleansed her eyes and caused her to see more clearly.

If you have ever studied physiology you will know that eyes are like glasses which need to be washed constantly, else they will not be transparent. Each time the eyelids close, tears flow forth to wash the eyes. In like manner, in the spiritual realm, if there are no tears, our spiritual eyes will not be washed; and so we shall be unable to see clearly. Those who have never been hurt, who have never encountered any unpleasant circumstance, who have never known anguish, vexation and oppression in spirit, are ignorant and undiscerning in many things.

There was once a couple who lived quite well before the Lord. They both were zealous and served the Lord well. After a short while, though, the child whom they loved dearly died. They became indignant, and declared: "Hereafter we will not serve God any more. We have served Him so faithfully, and yet He has allowed our child to die instead of blessing us." They indeed were no longer zealous and seeking as before, but spent their days carelessly for eight or nine years. One day while the father was walking in the wilderness he saw a shepherd trying to lead a flock through a creek. It was quite natural in the country for there to be no well-built bridge over the creek. Instead, a narrow board usually served as a bridge. Man could therefore dare to cross it, but for the sheep this was fairly difficult. They were both timid and dull. So that no matter how this shepherd coaxed and coerced, his sheep refused to cross the creek. Finally, the shepherd was driven to take the most precious lamb away from its mother and compel it to cross over by means of the board. The mother sheep, out of love for her baby lamb, ran the risk of crossing the creek on the board by following. With the result that all the rest of the flock crossed over to the other side of the creek too. Now when the father saw this, he wept, and then he exclaimed, "It is enough!" By this incident he was revived spiritually. Later he testified as follows: "For fear lest I would refuse to cross over and thus be left on this side of the creek, God took my child and brought him over first. If a foolish thing such as a sheep knows to follow through, why should *I* linger behind?" The father now saw clearly.

Frequently tears can bring people closer to God. A lack of such tears may be the reason why people who sail through life easily and comfortably—never suffering any deprivation—seldom have depth. All who are Christians during the time of prosperity but never during the day of tears cannot help but be ordinary, for they will not have had much experience. But then, many unbelievers have never believed in the Lord because they too have never suffered. They think they can live in this world by eating and drinking and making merry from dawn to dusk; if nothing special happens to them, they are able to get by throughout all their life. How, then, can they ever see light if they have never once shed tears? No wonder they are so foolish, deadly drunk with the world, and unsaved. O Christians, let us not harden our hearts—unwilling to wash our eyes with tears—lest we become dull and blind in spiritual things.

Let us now see what the Bible has to say about tears. Today I do not wish to counsel you to make merry but would counsel you to cry. And why? Because today is the time for weeping; this world is a place for mourning. Let me repeat that he who sets aside tears neither knows the time nor his place in the world. All who cannot shed tears have already lost their essential human character, because the true meaning of life is unquestionably expressed in tears. And as we look into the Scriptures may we be able to see what the Lord wants us to do. For throughout the entire Old and New Testaments there are innumerable times where tears are being mentioned. There will be no need for us to go through them all; a study of only a few of these Scriptures will be sufficient for our present purpose, which is, to deal with such points as the meaning of tears, the relationship of tears to a sinner's repentance, their relation to a believer's prayer and work, and finally, God's attitude towards tears.

A. *The Meaning of Tears*

Although tears sometimes flow forth out of sheer joy, usually they are caused by extreme sorrow or pressure beyond measure. Tears are shed because the sorrow, sadness, or pressure within us has become unbearable. Nevertheless, a most surprising thing happens at this juncture. As your tears flow, the many burdens within you are suddenly lightened. What was of tremendous importance before is now loosened up. It would appear as though something has gone out of you because of your tears. Otherwise, how could the many burdens inside you have been lessened? How could the pressure built up in you have decreased? Here may we see the meaning of tears. Tears discharge what is in the heart. Tears are the outlet of the heart. Let us search the Bible and take note of what it says about this matter.

"My friends scoff at me: but mine eye poureth out tears unto God" (Job 16.20). These were words spoken by Job after he had been assaulted by Satan and scoffed at by his three friends. Brethren, is this your experience, that you pour out tears before God when you are scorned and are oppressed by men? How often are you provoked by others? Have you ever been misunderstood and damaged? If you have encountered such things, did you cry as Job did? It is true that, before men, weeping is a sign of human weakness, but before God it is the proper thing to do. I often say that blessed is the man who has shed tears before God; because he who has never cried before God does not know what fellowship is, nor what it is to be near to God, nor how to cast a burden upon the Lord.

I have a friend who once told me something about tears. Said he: When your earthly path is blocked all around, when you are provoked on every side, when everybody accuses you of being wrong, and all your environment seems to revolt against you, then this is the time you should shed a few drops of tears before God; for this is your only way out, this alone can solve your problems. How very true are these words of my friend. And all who are experienced will say the same thing. If you wish to serve God faithfully and live godly, these things will come to you, and tears must flow. No believer can avoid such happenings. We may therefore declare that no one who is faithful has never shed any tears. Brothers and sisters, how about you? If you have told God your difficulty as well as your joy, I counsel you to offer your tears to Him too.

"Every night make I my bed to swim; I water my couch with my tears" (Ps. 6.6). David was in distress at that time. He was also physically ill. He wept every night till his bed was made to swim and his couch was wet all over. Forgive me my saying an unpleasant word, but I believe that all who can only laugh but never weep too are shallow and superficial. He who laughs and jokes all the day long betrays an emptiness within. For no one who has ever been dug up by God has failed to cry and weep. Tears express that which is inside a person, so that people are able to see what God has done in him. Yet what is indeed precious to God is not our tears shed in public to be seen by men but our secret tears which we shed for Him alone to see. "Tears unto God", tears of the night—these are the truly proper, precious tears. We know David was disposed to weeping. In the Psalms are a number of places which record his tears. Each time he fell into sin or distress he shed tears before God. Not so with Saul, though, who knew only to lose his temper and be angry but never to shed tears.

We have already seen how tears are expressive

of sorrow. We also know that sorrow creates deep feeling within, whereas our laughing touches the human heart very little. Laughter is somewhat superficial; but sorrow comes from within, and hence it enters deeply into another's heart. This is universally recognized by all who are well experienced in life. Genuine tears disclose a wounded heart, and in the presence of such tears the heart melts. But tears which flow without anguish of heart are meaningless.

David was brought by God into such depth and had so much experience because he shed many tears. The profusion of his tears showed the multitude of his sufferings and adversities. Many lessons were learned in distress, just as Romans indicates: "tribulation works endurance" (5.3 Darby). Let us understand that David became what he was partly because of his tears. Had there been no tears to develop him, he would not have been any deeper than the ordinary person.

When the children of Israel were taken captive and carried away to the nations, people ridiculed them by saying, "What do you have now? The temple of your God is destroyed; your country is fallen. Where then is your God? What has happened to you?" It was under such a circumstance as this that the sons of Korah wrote a very meaningful psalm, part of which runs as follows: "My tears have been my food day and night, while they continually say unto me, Where is thy God?" (42.3) At that time they really suffered, because people lashed out at them with very sharp words. They therefore had no other recourse but to shed tears before God. It is human nature to find opportunity to pierce and to hurt those whom we hate; people rejoice in another's suffering. Hence we find that the enemies of Israel pierced the hearts of the Israelites with reproaches and ridicule so as to make them suffer. So that all they could do was to shed tears. Later on, however, we discover how God greatly regarded those tears.

"Then I returned and saw all the oppressions that are done under the sun; and, behold, the tears of such as were oppressed, and they had no comforter; and on the side of their oppressors there was power; but they had no comforter" (Eccl. 4.1). In this verse we see how tears flow because of hearing unpleasant words, how distress and oppression produce grief and anxiety. Being pressed by these things for some time until you can no longer endure them, you will find that your tears begin to gush forth.

"She weepeth sore in the night, and her tears are on her cheeks; among all her lovers she hath none to comfort her: all her friends have dealt treacherously with her; they are become her enemies" (Lam. 1.2). Lamentations was written by Jeremiah, and it is a book which reveals the experiences of the children of Israel in their captivity. This particular verse from the book shows us that due to treacherous treatment given them by men, the children of Israel wept with many tears.

From these various Scripture passages quoted we realize that tears are the result of oppression, treachery, ridicule, and all kinds of adverse circumstances, that tears often indicate pressure and pain. And we know that all these things happened to our Lord, otherwise His heart would not have cried out in tears. His tears tell us how He endured these things. Hence the shedding of tears is not something to be ashamed of; on the contrary, it is something holy.

I would say that in this world tears excel the smile. This world full of sin and perversity is fortunate indeed to have a few drops of tears with which to wash itself; otherwise, this world would probably be far worse. It is fortunate, in this blind and wicked generation, to have a few warm tears to betoken one final trace of human feeling. Were there not even a few tears evident, this world would truly be darker than hell. Due to God's providential care, many beautiful flowers today are watered by tears in the form of rain-drops falling from heaven; or else they would all be withered.

The intimate relationships existing in this world between parents, husband and wife, brothers and sisters, and among near relatives are happily maintained by a few timely drops of tears; otherwise we would descend into living according to the conditions that shall mark the Great Tribulation. We know that the anti-Christ is someday coming; but today he is effectively restrained by tears. Without tears the sufferings on earth would undoubtedly be deepened and sin would be greatly increased. Tears, therefore, represent the true meaning of life. It shows that man has not yet completely abandoned his humanity but continues to retain a sense of sin. For where sin is present, there ought to be tears. Unhappy environment, sad event, and past recollection may all cause us to shed tears. Yet many have none to shed because they have forgotten their past history, forgotten their departure from the Garden of Eden, as well as forgotten their precarious standing today. So that in God's plan of redemption man will not be able to return to his original position if he has no tears. A person who forgets what he has gone through sheds no tears. Tears, then, are the symbol of painful recollection.

B. *The Effects of Tears*

1. Concerning Salvation

Tears are not something one can himself control. If a person can shed them whenever he wants to, then such tears have lost their meaning and value completely. If weeping does not issue out of the anguish of the heart, it has absolutely no significance and is purely counterfeit. Though tears are beyond anyone's own control, they nonetheless are everybody's share and hence everyone should have them shed. If someone professes to have never shed any tears, I believe he is a man without a heart and cannot be called a Christian.

Let me now speak a few words to any unbelieving friends who may be reading these pages. Do you know that tears may bring people to the Lord Jesus? that weeping may cause people to draw nearer to God in heaven? This is because tears can remove whatever hinders, that is to say, the tears of repentance drive away sin.

Friends, do you realize what sin is? Do you know what it will bring? And have you repented of sin even to the shedding of tears? If you have never felt sorry for your sin, I wonder whether you really have a heart. Anyone who can shed no tears for sin is, may I say, like a piece of wood or stone which has neither affection nor feeling. Whatever your heart attitude towards sin is, your eyes will express it. Oh, the many sins in this world! I do not believe I need to mention what we have sinned against God; if I were to speak just a little of that which we have sinned against other people, you would be convinced. Just consider all the offences we have ever committed against people. Of the people whom we have met—such as our parents, husbands or wives, brothers and sisters, relatives, friends, schoolmates, colleagues, and so forth—who can count the number of times we have transgressed against them, deceived them, or ill-treated them? We may be unrighteous in handling things, or we may be in arrears in our payments. All these are sins. Now if they are never settled, we cannot draw near to God.

How very grave the situation is. Do you recognize the seriousness of sin? You have sinned, you are now full of sin, and all these sins will bring you into the bottomless pit. Friends, repent and return! Let your tears wash you! It is true that the blood alone can wash away sin. This is indeed basic and primary, but there is that which is complementary though secondary—namely, tears. In other words, before God, sin is washed with the blood, but in the human heart it is cleansed by tears. It is quite true that before God, tears can never wash away sin, only the blood of the Lord can. Yet blood also demands tears. If the blood of the Lord is not accompanied by your tears, you have not really repented. The Lord's redemption without man's repentance and hatred of sin cannot wash away one's sin. In order to have subjective experience it is necessary to have tears. Let us observe what the ancients did.

"Their heart cried unto the Lord: O wall of the daughter of Zion, let tears run down like a river day and night; give thyself no respite; let not the apple of thine eye cease" (Lam. 2.18). Why did the Jews cry with tears? It was out of their repentance for their sin; and it was because Zion had been taken, Jerusalem occupied, and the people of Israel exiled to the east of the river Euphrates. At such a helpless moment they wept with tears for their sins, for the downfall of their nation, and for the destruction of the temple. I sincerely hope that today you would shed more tears and let your tears run down like a river day and night.

Oh that you, my unbelieving friend, would cry. He who can laugh at sin does not know what sin is, and neither does he know his destiny. One who has never shed tears is totally ignorant of the love of God and the preciousness of Christ. Anyone who fails to cry for sin fails to experience the joy of forsaking sin. To weep for sin is therefore indispensable. Have you done anything wrong to other people? Have you ever stolen somebody's article? Do you have pride, jealousy, or hatred? Unquestionably, we have sinned much against men as well as against God. And hence one thing is needful on our part, and that is, we need to have some tears. Not just a crying outwardly without feeling the pain in the heart, for that is futile. Tears are not primarily outward; their source must be in the heart. Only that which comes from the heart can ever move people as well as touch one's own self.

Yet shedding tears as a sign of repentance over sin is made even clearer in the New Testament. Read Luke 7.38 about the woman who, "standing behind at his [the Lord Jesus'] feet, weeping, . . . began to wet his feet with her tears, and wiped them with the hair of her head, and kissed his feet, and anointed them with the ointment." Whereupon the Lord said to Simon: "She hath wetted my feet with her tears, and wiped them with her hair" (v.44). Friends, may I ask if you have ever had this kind of tears? People in this world cry for various reasons: some cry because they suffer too much; some, because they hate too much; some, because they lose their temper in a quarrel. May I ask, though, if you have ever shed tears for your sin as did this woman?

Without any question the blood of the Lord cleanses all sin, but unless the blood is accompanied by man's tears it cannot be effective in man. Once Alexander the Great received a letter in which was listed one by one his mother's crimes. It was meant as an accusation of his mother before him. In reply, Alexander wrote but one sentence: "One drop of tears from my mother's eyes washes away all her crimes." And with that the matter was put to rest.

Of course, how ever much we shed tears, it cannot wash away a bit of our sin from before God. Nevertheless, the other side of the matter remains true: that in spite of the death of Jesus Christ, the efficacy of the blood will not come to us if there are no tears on our part. No one will accept the Lord and be saved without shedding the tears of repentance. Each one who truly believes in the Lord has the experience of repentance. A friend of mine once said that in reality there are two drugs for sin—one is the blood of the Lord, the other is our tears. Though this may sound strange, it is nonetheless true. In fact, no one who trusts in the blood has failed to shed tears. The typology in the Old Testament also bears this out. All who did not

get rid of whatever leaven they had, could not keep
the Passover; and all who did not eat unleavened
bread could not eat the flesh of the lamb. Hence
blood is of supreme importance, although it still
needs to be accompanied by man's warm penitent
tears in order for the blood to operate in man. We
as it were must take the Lord's blood in our hands
and mix it with a few drops of our tears. If a person
is not sorrowful for his past sin, he cannot be
saved.

Now let us turn our attention to the attitude of
the believer towards tears. We have noticed how
that woman wet the feet of the Lord with her tears.
It causes me to think that whenever we come
before the Lord, and even if we do not have the
money to buy ointment to anoint the head and feet
of the Lord, we each can nonetheless give Him our
tears. And we can thank God for that. For the
tears are as precious as the ointment. And how
much better it is to bring tears to the Lord than to
bring Him nothing. Hence let each of us bring his
warm tears to the Lord!

2. Concerning Prayer

"Hear my prayer, O Jehovah, and give ear unto
my cry; hold not thy peace at my tears: for I am a
stranger with thee, a sojourner, as all my fathers
were" (Ps. 39.12). Tearful prayer before God is the

best way to be heard. If tears are added to your prayer, it will be quickly answered. Many prayers are heartless because there are no tears. If you have heart, why not add your tears? Thus will you be able, as did the psalmist, to tell God: "I will not be long on this earth, for I am only a stranger and sojourner. It is miserable enough for me to be in this world, so please hear me." And God will surely hear our prayers. Though there is no merit in the tears themselves, yet they do express what is in your heart; that is to say, you really have a heart desire. May we therefore add more tears to our prayers that we may be heard.

"Turn back, and say to Hezekiah the prince of my people, Thus saith Jehovah, the God of David thy father, I have heard thy prayer, I have seen thy tears: behold, I will heal thee; on the third day thou shalt go up unto the house of Jehovah" (2 Kings 20.5). How good a word this is! God sees our tears! Hezekiah prayed to God for more days to live, and he also wept. And God answered him. This shows how the Lord is pleased with our tearful prayers; such prayers can move His heart. In view of this, then whatever matter which cannot move *your* heart to tears cannot move *God's* heart either. Hence it behooves us to shed more tears before the Lord. A weeping before men reveals your weakness, in that you lack the mien of a man; but a not weeping before God manifests that you are as numb as wood and stone.

I personally treasure very much this word in 2

Kings 20.5: "I have seen thy tears." Each time we meet a difficult situation which is heartbreaking, distressing, pressed beyond measure and with no way out, we can lift up our heads and drop a few tears before God, for He surely sees. Yet be clear of this, that tears are futile if they are not shed before God. Naturally, there are many people in this world who are prone to weeping. Man's cry simply expresses his own sorrow and distress; it in itself will not produce any positive result. Tears with prayer, however, *is* effective. Every time you cry in distress, why not add to it prayer? You may tell God your sorrow and distress through prayer. The Bible shows us not only the tearful prayer of Hezekiah but also the prayers and supplications of our Lord which came with strong crying and tears (see Heb. 5.7).

Oftentimes it is useless to cry to each other; but if one cries to God it is effective, since God sees one's tears and will hear one's prayer. Indeed, every drop of tears shed before God will be counted by Him—"Thou numberest my wanderings: put thou my tears into thy bottle; are they not in thy book?" (Ps. 56.8) Please note that such is the advantage of having tears before God. O sorrowful heart, if life makes you suffer, and you are pressed beyond measure, passing your days in misery, and weary in battling many problems, why not cry before God? Let me tell you, this will never never fail. God will record the tears you shed each time. He will put them in His bottle, which means

He will remember all your sufferings. Thank God, our tears do not fall to the ground and mix with the dust; rather, they are stored in God's bottle of remembrance; for are they not in His record-books? God will not forget; He will always remember our tears.

Let me ask you a question. Do you know what kind of cry is most comforting and satisfying? When does a child cry the loudest and strongest? It is not at the time when he is beaten nor when he is hungry, but at the first instance that he sees his dear mother at home after he has been insulted and troubled by people on the outside. At that moment he will cry very loud and very long. Oh, to cry before a lover is most consoling. There is neither meaning nor effect to cry before ordinary people. Where and when should we therefore cry? Undoubtedly before the God who cares most for us and who is the dearest to us. Let us cry our heart out before Him, for He treasures us. It is most comforting to cry before the Lord because He is listening and seeing. He will perform that which we ask for. Oh, we surely will reap the best consequence if we weep before God.

Let us further consider the advantage of tearful prayer as we look into the story recorded in Mark 9 of the father and the son. "Straightway the father of the child cried out, and said, I believe; help thou mine unbelief" (v.24). At that moment the father's heart was suffering greatly, and he hated himself for his unbelief. The father had witnessed the intense suffering of his child and had tried everything without result. And then he had asked the disciples of the Lord to help, but that too had been of no avail. He was therefore really desperate now. Under such anguish and anxiety, he could not help but cry out immediately to the Lord. And what was the outcome? The outcome was that the Lord heard his prayer, and the child was healed. We need to see that many prayers are ineffectual for the simple reason that there are no tears.

"How unceasing is my remembrance of thee in my supplications, night and day longing to see thee, remembering thy tears, that I may be filled with joy" (2 Tim. 1.3–4). Why did Paul long to see Timothy? Because of the tears of Timothy. In the Bible those who serve the Lord seem all to be persons who know how to weep. So that I believe that no one who serves the Lord well will be exempt from shedding tears. Tears appear to be a necessity to workers. It is therefore best if tears are mingled with prayer for God to remember and to hear.

3. Concerning the Lord's Work

Let us now see what is the relationship of tears to the work of the Lord. What is its place?

"Oh that my head were waters, and mine eyes a fountain of tears, that I might weep day and night for the slain of the daughter of my people!" (Jer.

9.1) Jeremiah wept often; hence he is called the weeping prophet. "And let them make haste, and take up a wailing for us, that our eyes may run down with tears, and our eyelids gush out with waters" (v.18). "But if ye will not hear it, my soul shall weep in secret for your pride; and mine eye shall weep sore, and run down with tears, because Jehovah's flock is taken captive" (13.17). If people did not listen to God's word, Jeremiah wept because of it. "And thou shalt say this word unto them, Let mine eyes run down with tears night and day, and let them not cease; for the virgin daughter of my people is broken with a great breach, with a very grievous wound" (14.17). He wept because the children of Israel were wounded. No one who faithfully serves the Lord in His word can keep away from tears. Indeed, anyone who sheds no tears for the work only proves that his heart is not on the work. All who have the work on their hearts cannot refrain from crying. Sometimes in dealing with a person, you have exhausted every method you know of and still you fail. Let me tell you this: that there is yet another means at your disposal—to shed tears. At those times when all other kinds of persuasion have been used without result, the last persuasion will be tears. When all kinds of weapons have been wielded without any victory, the last weapon to be used is tears. People may resist the other weapons, but in the presence of weeping they have to yield.

None who loves the Lord does not weep. Weep

with sympathy for sinners, weep with desire for the glory of God, and weep with eagerness to overcome the enemy. Of course, those who have no heart to please the Lord do not have such experience. But all whose hearts are on the Lord's work are bound to weep. Jeremiah was one of the prophets in the Old Testament greatly used by the Lord. He attained to such distinction because he shed many tears. He cared so much for the children of God that he cried day and night.

Without a doubt tears are something we must have, because this world is in great need of much tears by which to wash her. Many young believers need to be nurtured and disciplined with tears. Spiritual life needs to be maintained with tears. Numerous sinners need to have the seed of the gospel sown in their hearts with tears. Without weeping, nothing can be done. Today the Christian's consecration is not adequate. Many offer their bodies, strength, money, and time; yet they fail to offer their tears. No wonder many works are incomplete and untold numbers of believers are not nurtured.

If we shed tears for the work, what will be the outcome? Do be aware of this, that tears will not be shed forever, because there is a time for it to cease. For please note this verse: "Thus saith Jehovah: Refrain thy voice from weeping, and thine eyes from tears; for thy work shall be rewarded, saith Jehovah; and they shall come again from the land of the enemy" (Jer. 31.16). If we really shed tears for the work, God says we shall be rewarded.

One can easily stress the importance of tears in God's work when one notes its significance in the family. Look at how a mother treats a child. I have never seen a good mother who only gets anxious but never cries over the bad conduct of her child. Among Christians the tears shed by mothers for their children are most effectual. The coming home of a prodigal depends largely on the tears of the mother. However bad and far away a prodigal may be, he will soon be brought back if a good mother at home is weeping for him. What can anxiety, strife, and punishment exhibited by the mother accomplish for a bad child if there are no tears in the mother? A woman may possess all the virtues, but she is not a good mother if she lacks tears. So too, in our work of dealing with sinners or young believers, tears are also necessary. To seek out a young brother, to help him, and to read the Bible with him—all these measures are profitable; yet they are not complete without that which Jeremiah had prayed for; namely, "Oh that mine eyes were a fountain of tears." It is good for many who serve the Lord to ask God for utterance, power, knowledge, opportunity, and so forth; still, one thing must not be lacking in the Lord's work, and that is, "Let mine eyes run down with tears."

Such an example for us is not only to be found in the Old Testament but in the New Testament as well: "Serving the Lord with all lowliness of mind, and with tears" (Acts 20.19); "Wherefore watch ye, remembering that by the space of three years I ceased not to admonish every one night and day with tears" (v.31). How did Paul serve the Lord? He served with all lowliness of mind and with tears night and day. Shedding tears is therefore a good way to work. Let me say again that no one is perfect who does not shed tears. Though he may do quite well in many things, he is not reckoned as perfect if he has no tears. In serving the Lord we must add to it our tears (which are to be shed before both the Lord and men). Yet this is not something put on; rather, it is the spontaneous outcome of a heart that has been deeply moved.

Paul asked the elders of the church in Ephesus to remember how for three years he had served them with tears. May I ask if you too have shed tears in this manner for the work? In order to ascertain whether one is zealous and single-minded in the Lord's work, one needs only to inquire if he has wept. Frankly speaking, a work will never prosper without weeping. The lack of this one thing done in secret will hinder the success of the work.

"Out of much affliction and anguish of heart I wrote unto you with many tears; not that ye should be made sorry, but that ye might know the love which I have more abundantly unto you" (2 Cor. 2.4). We all know that the first letter to the Corinthians was written after Paul had heard from the household of Chloe as to the conditions of the Corinthian believers. In that letter he had pointed

out to them their many errors, and had reprimanded them with the most straightforward and
severest of words. Here in the second letter,
though, Paul tells how he had written that first
letter. It had been written out of much affliction
and anguish of heart with many tears.

When you hear the fall of any brother or sister,
do *you* weep with much tears as did Paul? Without
question the shedding of tears is not an easy thing.
If it requires some strength to laugh, it needs far
more strength to shed tears. Do you have the
strength to weep? Notice in Paul's writing to the
Corinthians how severe were his words. They cut
through like a sword. Said Paul, "Put away the
wicked man from among you" or else. Such words
do indeed cut deeply. One thing is quite certain,
however; which is, that if you want your words to
wound others, let those same words first wound
you; for without you being pierced by those words
yourself, those words of yours will not be able to
pierce others. Paul was truly this kind of person.
When he uttered these most heavy and cutting of
words in the first letter, he had in reality uttered
them with tears. Before ever his words had been
spoken and other people had begun to feel the
pain, he himself had suffered first. Let us therefore
recognize that people themselves should suffer first
before they can cause others to suffer. Nothing will
be accomplished if they only make other people
suffer.

For this reason, each one who works for the

Lord must have experience in tears. Whenever you see a brother fall or defeated you are not worthy to do the Lord's work nor worthy to either reprimand or persuade if you shed no tears. Before you chide a brother or a sister, before you tell him his error, you first must be afflicted and hurt by the sharpness of the words to be spoken. Only in this way are you qualified. How easy it is to speak of people's weakness, but how hard to speak it with tears. Yet only the person who has tears is ever really qualified to speak.

Thank God, the blood of His Son once fallen to the ground has never turned back, so that people may still be saved through its efficacy. Thank God, too, that the *tears* of His Son have not turned back either, so that we today may know His heart of concern and learn to shed tears before God and men. Let us follow the footsteps of our Lord and shed some more tears in our prayer and work.

"They that sow in tears shall reap in joy. He that goeth forth and weepeth, bearing seed for sowing, shall doubtless come again with joy, bringing his sheaves with him" (Ps. 126.5,6). Are you thinking of witnessing for the Lord? This verse tells you how you should do it. For the seed here is the gospel, and the sheaves are the saved souls. The seed you sow needs to be watered with your tears in order for it to grow. Without water the seed will not grow. Do not imagine that it is easy to bear fruit; it takes tears to be successful in such fruit-bearing. What is said here is that if you shed tears secretly before God, you will with rejoicing bring some sheaves home. How frequently we make the preaching of the gospel common. No wonder the seed neither grows nor ripens. Tears are closely related to work. Whatever work lacks tears, it is bound to end in failure, because tears represent your heart. Where your tears are, there also is your heart. This is an indisputable fact. May we be zealous and let the tears run down for God's work.

C. *What God Will Do to Our Tears*

Let us now see how God will treat our tears. "Thou numberest my wanderings: put thou my tears into thy bottle; are they not in thy book?" (Ps. 56.8) God does remember; He numbers our tears. He never forgets one drop of them even.

"Thou hast fed them with the bread of tears, and given them tears to drink in large measure" (Ps. 80.5). "Thou hast delivered my soul from death, mine eyes from tears, and my feet from falling" (Ps. 116.8). God seems to give us tears to drink and to eat. In fact, our whole life on earth is spent in tears. We make tears our companion. How this world is a land of tears. Almost every square foot of red earth is wet with tears. It in effect can be said that no place is dry. For everything here on earth is able to make us cry; every circumstance will pierce our heart. There is no peace on earth.

Only hurt is the situation here. God, however, will deliver our eyes from tears and our feet from falling. And this day will soon come; we will not live forever in such a tearful world.

"And God shall wipe away every tear from their eyes" (Rev. 7.17). The people in view here are "they that come out of the great tribulation, and they washed their robes, and made them white in the blood of the Lamb" (v.14b). God shall wipe away every tear from their eyes. This is the Lord's promise given before the millennial kingdom.

"And he shall wipe away every tear from their eyes; and death shall be no more; neither shall there be mourning, nor crying, nor pain, any more: the first things are passed away" (Rev. 21.4). After the millennial kingdom the Lord also promises all the saved ones that He will wipe away their tears.

I delight greatly in the New Jerusalem. Not because it has the street of pure gold and twelve gates of pearl, but because there is the presence of the Lord and the absence of any more tears there. If we die today, it is not for vexation but for rest, just as we might lie down to sleep a while after having become tired of walking. However, we all are waiting for that day of no more tears to come, we are not waiting for death. People like Paul have rested for about two thousand years. Some of us may go to rest today. Yet should the Lord tarry longer, the remainder of us may have our earthly days prolonged to thirty or fifty years. Even so, thanks be to God that that day *is* coming, this world *shall* weep no more.

The Lord has borne our pain so that we may not suffer again in the future. Thank God, there shall be no more pain for there is no more sin. Trouble, pain, and tears arise from sin, but there shall not be any sin any more, and hence, no more tears forever. Praise God, the days of sorrow will not last long, the New Jerusalem is coming soon, and this tearful world shall instantly pass away. Oh the wonder of it, that on *that* side all pains are gone because all sin is taken away.

On that day the Lord will give us a resurrection body. I think that that body will be similar to ours today, possessing all the different members that our body has today; yet it will be a transformed body. And in this transformed body one thing shall be missing—the tears in the eyes. For you see, tears are something for the night; and hence, there will be no more need of them, since night will be done away.

How blessed we are. This earthen vessel of ours shall not work and pray on earth forever. As long as we are still here, we are satisfied with God. But, this will not be for long. Oh, that day is coming. And how I wish that day to come quickly.

In conclusion, then, let me end with a story. Towards the end of the First World War a battlefield was full of heavily wounded soldiers, both French and German. A wounded Frenchman gave a wounded German a drink of water out of his bottle. They were both Christians, and both were dying. After the German soldier finished drinking, the French soldier took his hand and said, "There shall be no more war over there." And with that they both collapsed and died. Let me too say today that over there, there shall be no more tears.

2 Mastering Temper

After a believer has received the grace of the Lord, his conduct and personality ought to undergo certain changes. One of those changes is related to his temper. It is most pathetic to observe many whose temper remains unchanged after they have believed in the Lord for a number of years. This brings much dishonor to the Lord. One should therefore have his temper problem solved immediately after he is saved. He should not allow his bad temper to continue in him without any drastic change occurring for some years after he has believed.

Certain Expressions of the Christian Life

There are certain distinctive expressions of the Christian life which a person should exhibit after he has trusted the Lord.

The Lord commanded His disciples to "love one another" (John 15.12). One expression of a Christian life is love. We ought to love people. We must love all men as well as love our brethren.

The Lord himself also said: "Blessed are the meek" (Matt. 5.5). A Christian's attitude should be one of meekness, not arrogance. We ought to learn to be meek and lowly, for our Lord's demeanor is gentle—"Behold, thy King cometh unto thee, meek, and riding upon an ass" (Matt. 21.5).

Further, in Luke we are told: "If any man would come after me, let him deny himself, . . . and follow me" (Luke 9.23). A Christian's life is one of self-denial. He does not speak for himself, nor does he strive for his own self. Instead of building up himself, he denies himself.

"Beareth all things" (1 Cor. 13.7). A Christian's life is not overbearing but bearing all things. "Rejoice always" (1 Thess. 5.16). A Christian's life should be joyful. He must not permit anything to disturb his peace. God's children must maintain their peace continuously.

Matthew 11.29 is also very significant, for the Lord himself there says: "I am meek and lowly in heart." A Christian should be humble. A Christian's attitude should not be haughty but one of humility.

Losing Temper Is Inconsistent with Christian Living

The love, meekness, self-denial, bearing, joy, peace, and humility which we have just mentioned are all the normal expressions of a Christian life. It is therefore evident that the loss of temper is incompatible with these expressions.

Where love is, there is not ill-temper. No one can express love on the one hand and be out of temper on the other. The Lord's command to us Christians is to love people, whether believers or non-believers. Should love fill your heart, harsh temper is dispelled from you. You should see how important it is for a child of God to love others. Love must become your disposition as well as your action. It is not just for you to love once or twice; love is your constant attitude. This being the case, you have no way to lose your temper.

The Lord charges us to be meek. How meek He was while on earth. He rode upon an ass to show that His kingship is not based upon sternness but meekness. During His earthly days He was One who could be easily talked to, easily invited, and easily approached. Some people are difficult to talk with; but a Christian should not be so; instead, he should be one who is easy to be approached. A Christian ought to be a meek person. If we are meek in our disposition as well as in our attitude, we will just naturally not lose our temper. For all the outbursts of temper are ill-mannered, being the rudest of human emotions; whereas the most delicate of all man's emotions is love or kindness. A person who is meek before the Lord leaves no ground for harsh temper. He who easily loses his temper or is quarrelsome expresses the roughest of emotions, which is totally incongruous with meekness.

The Lord exhorts us to deny ourselves. He wants us to learn to be self-denying people. It is obvious that a man who is willing to deny himself and to lay down his personal rights will not lose his temper. The reason for losing temper is self-seeking. If a person does not strive for himself, he will hardly lose his temper. We who are children of God ought to deny rather than preserve ourselves.

Sometimes people are really unreasonable towards us and many things done to us are truly irritating, but the Bible informs us that love "is not provoked" (1 Cor. 13.5). And the Lord shows us at the same time that we ought to bear with one another. If the Lord allows anything to come our way, He will certainly enable us to bear with it. The Lord's command is that our Christian life be a life of patience and endurance. If we endure, there is no possibility of losing our temper.

A Christian should always rejoice, for joy is life. How can a person be in a fit of temper and in the meanwhile be joyous? Such a combination is absolutely impossible. Either you are joyful or you are in a bad temper. You cannot be joyous and lose control of your temper at the same time. If the joy of the Lord should fill your heart, you will give no place to ill-temper in your life. The Lord leaves no ground for us to get into a temper. Were our lives full of joy, our bad temper would naturally fall away.

The Lord wants us to have our hearts filled with peace. He desires that nothing whatsoever may disturb our peace and that we may retain peace in everything. The peace of the Lord will garrison or guard our hearts and minds so as to keep them from being assaulted (see Phil. 4.7). Should our hearts truly be full of peace as we have just stated, there can be no possibility of getting into a fit of temper.

We, the children of God, are humble people. God has not called us to be arrogant, neither has He inspired us to seek high places. On the contrary, His Son lived humbly on earth. God's will for us is that we be humble and condescend towards the humble. Losing one's temper is incompatible with humility. We should learn to follow the humble Lord in this humble way.

"Every one who is angry with his brother [many ancient authorities insert 'without cause'] shall be in danger of the judgment" (Matt. 5.22). The Lord does not like His people to lose their temper and become angry without cause. To be angry with a brother is especially unbecoming. A child of God should learn not to lose control of his temper and not to get angry easily.

The Root of Losing Temper: Self

The losing of temper is a common problem shared by many people. We must recognize that this is a highly superficial problem which ought to be solved shortly after one is saved. It should not take eight or ten years to discover how one's temper is out of control. If so, then why do so many people lose their temper? And why is this problem unsolved in the lives of many Christians? Without a proper answer, we shall find no way to be good Christians. We need to understand why a person is so prone to lose his temper, and thus we may know how to solve this problem.

This matter of losing one's temper is a considerably big problem to us, yet in the Bible we are not even able to find the word "temper". What we view as a most common fault seems to be ignored completely in the Bible. Why? Because *the losing of temper is a symptom, not a disease.* Disease and symptom are two different things. A person may have appendicitis—and this is a disease. His fever runs high—but this is a symptom. The symptom is caused by the disease. It is futile to treat only the symptom without treating the disease as well. The fever may subside temporarily, but it will return if the disease is still present. Losing control of temper is not a disease, it is a symptom. Hence we must search out the source of the disease. If the root is found and eliminated, the symptom will quite naturally disappear. Should we mistake the loss of temper as a disease, we miss the way; and no wonder, then, that we cannot solve the problem.

Many brethren confess that Romans 6.11 is problematic in their lives due to this matter of losing the temper. It is said in Romans 6.11 that we must reckon ourselves to be dead; but many find difficulty in applying this scripture verse. During an outburst of temper many try hurriedly to repeat Romans 6.11, saying "I am dead"; though "if I were dead," they say afterwards, "I could not have lost my temper." Such recital produces no result. For Romans 6.11 is not meant to relieve the symptom, rather is it meant to remove the disease. It will not be effective if it is used on a symptom. To reckon oneself dead during a fit of temper will not stop the outburst. Even if it may suppress temper from bursting forth, it still will not prevent temper from boiling within.

What, then, is the root of the disease which causes the symptom of losing the temper? There is a simple answer: losing the temper has to do with one's "self". A person's search for a solution ends at the wrong place if he does not deal with his own self but instead thinks of dealing with his temper. He loses his temper because of his own self. *That self of his is his disease*, his temper is not at all his disease. Due to the fact of this self, there is the outburst of such temper. If his self is being dealt with before God, his temper will naturally fade away. For this reason, the Bible pays attention to the self rather than to the temper. Were the problem of self solved, the problem of temper would automatically be solved also. If the basic problem of self is not solved, the secondary problem of temper will not be solved either.

As to this "self", let us look into several of its characteristics. *First*, some people are highly subjective. A subjective person must be full of self. He has his opinion on every matter, and he has his conviction on every subject. He considers his own opinion and conviction as infallible. And he insists on seeing his own idea adopted. He cannot tolerate any obstruction or frustration or rejection. His view must be accepted and his opinion must be carried through. If on any day his opinion is not respected and his view not adopted, his subjectiveness is unable to bear with it. And what will be the outcome? He will lose his temper and be thrown into a fit.

Oh dear friends, you are always attentive to your temper, and therefore you cannot cure the disease. The real disease is your subjectiveness. It lies in your stubborn will, not in your temper. When your subjective attitude is broken and your opinion and view are mortally wounded, you will then say to the Lord, "Lord, this is of Your doing and I submit." Will you be able to lose your temper after that? As your opinion is being shattered, you will kneel down and say, "Lord, this is Your business. Lord, this is Your act." Can you then be angry with anybody? There is no possibility to get angry.

The reason why our temper gets out of control is because we are determined to carry through with our own opinion and idea. We have conceived a set of plans which must be carried out. Our "self" comes out, and so our temper flares up. No one is able to be ill-tempered if his "self" has already been dealt with. For the source of bad temper is the self. It is rather foolish to spend time on dealing with temper while forgetting to deal with the self. As soon as we believe in the Lord, we should learn the lesson of brokenness: My own self is not worth preserving before the Lord, my self has no lingering value in His presence. Though baffled and tried on all sides, I will not lose my temper if there is no "self" in operation.

Second, some people lose their temper because they deem themselves to be extraordinary and look upon themselves as superior. In short, they are proud. The proud not only think highly of their own selves but also desire others to admire them and look up to them. They are never satisfied with their speaking good of themselves; they want other people to praise them too. In other words, the "self" of the proud will not stop at themselves but will try to extend such self-exaltation through others. They wish to be admired and exalted by all the brothers and sisters. If any brother should come to them and fail to discover how valuable and important they are, or what spiritual position or high spirituality they have, they will feel hurt and their temper will break lose. What causes the temper? Pride of self. People show bad temper because they are proud. *If you get rid of your pride you will get rid of your temper.* How impossible it is to try getting rid of your temper without getting rid of your pride. *The root of temper is pride.*

If you are a humble person before God, and if you realize that the ridicule, despising, and slander which come from people are parts of the discipline of the Holy Spirit, you will accept such discipline, saying: "O Lord, You are always for my good. All these things come to me that my pride may be dealt with. Lord, I thank You for edifying me with these things." Then you will not lose control of your temper. Even if, for example, a brother should disobey you and damage your position, you know you should not be proud but will instead say to the Lord: "Lord, You are right in dealing with my pride." You learn to recognize the hand of the Lord, and thus you will not lose your temper.

Let us realize that the losing of temper is not a disease. If you deal with it as you would deal with a disease, you will certainly fail. You should learn to fall down before the Lord and say, "Lord, You may do anything You like with me." When you put your self aside, willing to deny it and to deal with it, you shall see that during these days you seem to have lost the strength to get thrown into a temper. You have no desire to go into a fit and your temper has relinquished its control over you.

Third, in the very concept of self-exaltation is the thought that no one else could be as high as one's own self. A person will expect himself to rise higher while expecting others not to rise at all. He anticipates gain for himself but not for other people. He rejoices at others' failure and grieves at peoples' success. This concept is called jealousy. Such jealousy is evident in spiritual affairs as well as in worldly affairs. The proud is pleased with his brother's fall but is unhappy with his brother's progress. Such an attitude is the meanest of all attitudes; there is no mentality lower than this one. If a person delights in another's fall, he shares the attitude of Satan, for Satan loves to see people fall. How shameful it is for God's children to harbor Satan's feeling! To be happy rather than burdened over the stumbling of a brother is the most despicable and vilest of all feelings.

Yet what causes such a feeling? It is the craving for self-exaltation. He wishes everybody around him to falter but he alone to stand high up. Yet the one who knows God should expect other people to be raised up as well as his own self. But the one who does not know God would only hope for his own exaltation and not that of others. Worse than that, he even wishes others to *fall* so that he may appear to be higher. This kind of attitude is very base, for the source of many outbursts of temper lies in the jealousy within the heart. If you are one who exalts your own self, you will grow angry when you meet someone better and higher than you are. Jealousy stirs up the temper. You and I will never succeed if we forget to deal with jealousy and only deal with the temper. We must eliminate jealousy from our heart before we can ever control our temper. As long as the spirit of jealousy remains, there will be the breaking out of temper.

Fourth, some people show their self in another area—that is, self-love, the loving of one's own self. Among so many people, the one he loves most will be his own self. The center of attention and affection is himself. He considers himself to be the most important person in eating and lodging and in all the affairs of life. He hopes his profit will increase, and that he will be more comfortable. All his thoughts are woven around his own self. He is aware of only himself and treasures himself dearly. If he encounters anything that would cause discomfort to him, he will respond with an outbreak of temper. Many lose their temper because their self-love is wounded. A person who loves himself so very much will be most reluctant to have himself suffer a little loss, pain, or difficulty. In case anyone should hurt his self-love and cause him some discomfort or loss, he will be set on fire and burst into a fit of temper. But for a man who has been instructed of God, he knows that he lives for the Lord and he lives by the grace of God, not by his self-love. It is God's grace, not his self-love, that sustains him and makes him stand. However much may be the reason to become angry, he will not be so because his self-love has already been dealt with. May you and I see that all tempers are produced by the self. If the self has not been dealt with, the temper will cling to us. How can we possibly expect to have control over our temper if we ourselves are not being dealt with?

Fifth, some brothers and sisters love themselves to such a degree that they look only to their own things and have no concern or interest for the things of others. They have no desire to help other people. All their deeds and thoughts are centered upon their own selves. They themselves are the most important persons in the world, and their affairs are the most urgent. For a person whose thoughts and deeds are all for himself and who is always busily occupied with his own self, how will he have the leisure for other people? If someone should come and seek him out too much, he will feel annoyed, and his temper will break out. This is because all his activities are centered on himself, so that he has no sympathy for anybody else. He loves his own self so much that he has no time to sympathize with other people. He is so busy with himself that he has no strength to bear the sufferings of others. Many lose their temper simply because of the intrusion by others upon their self-centered love. They are irritated, agitated, and therefore blow up.

Hence the root of temper lies in man's self. If we did not make ourselves the center, we would be able to sympathize with others and to learn to love people. We would then quite naturally not feel disturbed at all when we are bothered. We take interest in helping people, knowing that this is one service to God. Let us therefore never deal only with the temper, since the root of the trouble is not there. We must deal with the root which is self. If man's self is properly treated, the problem of temper is solved automatically. The more completely the problem of the self is solved, the greater the problem of the temper is resolved.

Sixth, some people not only love their own selves, they also have another kind of love, which is, that they love things, they love money. This kind of people has never been delivered from things or wealth. To them goods and money are precious. Their "self" is a self which loves material things. Their self is expressed in loving these things. If any one thing belonging to such a person should be overturned, broken, or lost by other people, he cannot keep back his temper. His self is being wounded, his love of things is being hurt; therefore, he is bound to blow up.

Yet the cause for his temper resides in himself, not in other people. For example, if with your hand you hit a piece of wood, what sound do you hear? The sound of wood. If you beat the wall, what sound do you hear? The sound of the wall. Or if you strike a glass, what sound do you hear? The sound of glass. The same hand, the same hit, but different sounds. For the wood will give out the wood sound; the wall, the wall sound; and the glass, the glass sound. Their sounds are different because their substances are different. Outward phenomena betray the inward nature of things. Turning back to the subject before us, then, we can see that our temper resides in *us*, not in the environment. If there were no self within us, no circumstance could induce us to lose our temper. The reason for losing our temper lies in the fact that there is still self in us. With the presence of self still there, the temper will burst forth whenever the self is served with a proper environment. Environment does not create temper, it only brings out the temper that was already in us.

To sum up, then, temper comes from within one's self. Whoever loses his temper only proves that one specific area or several areas of his self has or have not been dealt with. Whether or not the problem of the temper is solved depends on how much one's self is being dealt with before God. The deeper his self is taken care of, the greater is his deliverance from temper. If his self is not dealt with, his temper will remain with him. Do not be so foolish as to treat the temper only. Let us always remember that the problem of self is much deeper than that of the temper. With self left undealt with, the matter of the temper will never be solved. In the process of learning, we receive enlightenment which causes us to see, on the one hand, the actual conditions of our "self", and, on the other hand, God's mercy in making all sorts of arrangements in our circumstances. When things begin to come to us, one after another, and if we have learned anything before God, we will bow our heads and say to the Lord: "Lord, what You have arranged is the best. Your way in dealing with my self is the best. I submit and I accept." Thus shall we find the impossibility of losing the temper.

Contrariwise, though, if we do not recognize the hand of the Lord—just as the senseless mule does not recognize the hand of its master—we will consider everything to be of man or of environment. And hence our eyes will be upon man or environment, and so we will fret and fume. We will resist and remonstrate by reacting with anger. If a person does not treat the self but thinks of treating the temper alone, he will be disappointed. He needs to see that the root of the outburst of temper lies in the self. For a Christian to lose his temper, it simply reveals his resistance to the discipline of the Holy Spirit. He shows that he is unhappy with the arrangement which the Holy Spirit has ordered for him. Consequently, let us learn to accept the discipline of the Holy Spirit and learn to put ourselves aside, seeing how useless we are. Then shall the problem of temper naturally be solved.

As soon as we believe in the Lord we should attack this problem of the temper. We should not allow this problem to remain until we begin to tackle it several years later. As Christians we must be self-denying people, not being subjective, proud, jealous, self-loving, self-regarding or money-loving. We ought to realize how we must deny our "self". We should also learn to accept the discipline of the Holy Spirit, recognizing that all things which happen to us are arranged by the Holy Spirit for our good. Do not deal with temper, which is only a symptom; instead, deal with the self, which is the disease. We cannot deal with an outburst of temper and not deal with the self. For where temper is, there is always the self. No one may excuse himself by saying that he is prone to an outburst of hot temper because his temperament is quick. Do not be deceived into thinking that the slow in temperament do not lose their temper. They can lose control of their temper just the same, though it may come forth in a different form. Wherever the self is, there the temper is. In order not to lose our temper we must deal with this self of ours. And as we are enlightened concerning this self of ours, we eventually will be delivered from our temper.

3 Idle Words Leak Life

He that guardeth his mouth keepeth his life; but he that openeth wide his lips shall have destruction. (Prov. 13.3)

A gentle tongue is a tree of life; but perverseness therein is a breaking of the spirit. (Prov. 15.4)

Ye offspring of vipers, how can ye, being evil, speak good things? for out of the abundance of the heart the mouth speaketh. . . . And I say unto you, that every idle word that men shall speak, they shall give account thereof in the day of judgment. For by thy words thou shalt be justified, and by thy words thou shalt be condemned. (Matt. 12.34,36,37)

If a waterpot has a hole, all the water in it will leak out. This is not a matter of whether there is water, rather is it a question of whether there is a

leak. Some brothers and sisters seem to really seek
the Lord in knowing the cross. Sometimes they are
quite willing to bear the cross. By all indications
they should be full of life. Yet, strangely, in such
people as these, who seek and admire and even
bear the cross, you cannot touch life. On the
contrary, you meet death. What is the cause for
such a strange situation? The answer is: the life
which they have received has all drained away.

"He that guardeth his mouth keepeth his life;
but he that openeth wide his lips shall have
destruction" (Prov. 13.3). We dare not rule dog-
matically either way that when Solomon wrote
this proverb he was referring to physical life or to
spiritual life. But we may take its principle and
apply it to the spiritual realm. This word shows us
one thing, which is, that a person who seeks the
Lord and who desires to supply the church with the
life he receives must be careful in word. If he is not
careful in word his life will leak away. Why is it
that some people are not of much use in God's
hand? It is because there has been a leakage of life.
You can only touch death and not life in them
because life has been drained away through their
words. Because of this, we need to guard our
mouth—and guard it vigilantly—before the Lord.
Many stories can be told how an idle word drains
away life more than does anything else. This does
not imply that sin is better than an idle word. But
we can say that aside from sin what dissipates life
most is our idle word.

"Every idle word that men shall speak, they shall give account thereof in the day of judgment" (Matt. 12.36). Does the Lord here speak of an unclean word? No. Does He here speak of a slanderous word? Not at all. Of an evil word? Again, the answer is no. What is spoken of here is an *idle* word. Idle words are superfluous words, irrelevant words, unnecessary words, or words of rumor which cause dispute. "They shall give account thereof in the day of judgment. For by thy words thou shalt be justified, and by thy words thou shalt be condemned" (v.36b,37). This is what the Lord Jesus has said. May we see the seriousness of *idle* words as well as slanderous words. Not only the speaking of unclean words is grave, the speaking of idle words is also of solemn significance. In the case of certain things and particular sins we are able to make some kind of restitution; but there are other things and other sins which cannot be recompensed at all. How can you make amends for idle words spoken against people? You may go to the person and confess your sin, you may say to that person that you take back your words; but their sound has already entered people's ears and no way is available to eliminate it. You may reimburse someone for things stolen, but by what means can you repay the damage done through idle words? Such a sin will be presented before God. Hence the Lord says: "Every idle word that men shall speak, they shall give account thereof in the day of judgment. For by thy words thou shalt be justified, and by thy words thou shalt be condemned."

"A gentle tongue is a tree of life; but perverseness therein is a breaking of the spirit" (Prov. 15.4). "Gentle" is a not being overheated; it is being moderate and proper in tone. With much speaking, the tongue becomes heated; and when the tongue gets overheated, there is no more tree of life. Only a *gentle* tongue is a tree of life. A gentle tongue is one that is neither hasty nor foolish nor babbling. Such a tongue is like a tree of life. You cannot smell the fragrance of Christ in a Christian who loves to chatter with idle words. He who delights in speaking idly is unable to supply others with life. For an idle word is but the creation of a big opening through which your life is leaked away.

Knowing that an idle word is a dissipation of life, what should we do about it? In order to guard our mouth we need first to deal with our heart. "For out of the abundance of the heart the mouth speaketh," says the Lord. The mouth utters whatever is in the heart. If you have something in your heart, your mouth sooner or later will express it. If you do not say it here, you will say it there: if not in this house, then it will be in another house. What the heart is filled with, that the mouth will spill out. Consequently, learning not to say idle words before God must begin with the dealing of the heart. If your heart is not dealt with, neither will your mouth ever be dealt with. For out of all the various things that fill the heart the mouth speaks them forth. Never excuse yourself by saying that you are a person who speaks without your heart being in it. Judging by the word of the Lord Jesus, there simply is no such possibility. With the mouth comes the heart. The mouth merely expresses what is in the heart. Hence the heart must be dealt with before the mouth can truly be dealt with.

Due to problems among the brethren at Corinth, Paul exhorted them by saying, "Speak the same thing" (1 Cor. 1.10a). How could they ever come around to speaking the same thing? By being "perfected together in the same mind and in the same judgment" (v.10b). The life of the church is similar to the life of an individual. As the life of an individual may be drained away through speaking idle words, so the life of the church also can be drained away through idle words. Since we have the same life, let us be of one mind and of one judgment. If so, we will be able to speak the same thing and be kept from speaking idle words. Let us therefore deal with the heart so that the mouth may also be dealt with.

"Doth the fountain send forth from the same opening sweet water and bitter?" (James 3.11) If a fountain cannot spill out two different kinds of water, how can a mouth spill out two different kinds of speech? As a fountain only sends forth one kind of water, so the mouth should only speak one kind of language. We need to deal specifically with idle words; for if this drainage is not stopped, what should not flow in will constantly come in through the one end and what should not flow out will continuously do so through the other end. And such a loss would be incalculable. Hence this leakage must be stopped. Let us ask the Lord: "Lord, deal with my mouth that it may be guarded through Your grace."

Furthermore, you must not only deal with your own mouth, you need also to deal with the other person's mouth. You should help those who are lovers of idle talk, those who love to babble and spread rumors. When such people come to you with the intention of saying many idle words, do not let them start. You may tell them: "Brother, let us pray." You will lead them in the right path by not letting them speak idly but leading them to either pray or recite Bible verses. You may even be so blunt as to suggest: "Brother, let us learn to say things that edify. It is better not to speak idle words."

Yet, to have the leak completely stopped we must first ask God to deliver us from our own curiosity so that we may learn to fear Him. Many Christians are so full of curiosity that they are eager to hear strange and even unclean stories. Their ears are like a garbage can into which all kinds of things can be dumped. If we are delivered from this curiosity, we will sin less, and likewise help our brothers and sisters to commit less sins. If our ears are not itching and if we give no opportunity to people to speak idle words, we will be able to keep our own mouth right before God so that it will not drain away life and will help to stop the leakage in others as well.

May we ask God to save us from idle words which dissipate life. Besides sin, an idle word too is a leak of life. Yet if we are kept in word in the right way, our life will not suffer loss. There will be no escape of life.

4 God Speaks through Environment

And God said unto Jacob, Arise, go up to Bethel, and dwell there: and make there an altar unto God, who appeared unto thee when thou fleddest from the face of Esau thy brother. Then Jacob said unto his household, and to all that were with him, Put away the foreign gods that are among you, and purify yourselves, and change your garments: and let us arise, and go up to Bethel; and I will make there an altar unto God, who answered me in the day of my distress, and was with me in the way which I went. And they gave unto Jacob all the foreign gods which were in their hand, and the rings which were in their ears; and Jacob hid them under the oak which was by Shechem. And they journeyed: and a terror of God was upon the cities that were round about them, and they did not pursue after the sons of Jacob. So Jacob came to Luz, which is in the land of Canaan

(the same is Bethel), he and all the people that were with
him. And he built there an altar, and called the place
El-bethel; because there God was revealed unto him,
when he fled from the face of his brother. And Deborah
Rebekah's nurse died, and she was buried below Bethel
under the oak; and the name of it was called Allonba-
cuth. (Gen. 35.1–8)

And Jacob said to Simeon and Levi, Ye have
troubled me, to make me odious to the inhabitants of
the land, among the Canaanites and the Perizzites: and,
I being few in number, they will gather themselves
together against me and smite me; and I shall be
destroyed, I and my house. (Gen. 34.30)

One

No matter what the degree of spiritual stature
one may attain, he still needs environment at times
to speak to him. There are instances of this nature
found both in the Old and the New Testaments. As
we read church history and study the experiences
of those who followed the Lord, we cannot unearth
one person who is never in need of circumstances
to speak a word to him. On the contrary, we may
confidently assert that there is no one who does not
need to be reminded sometimes by environment.
Many incidents convince us that the more spiritual
a person is before the Lord, the more that one will
permit environment to speak to him. Only those
who have controversy with the Lord will be easily
affected by circumstances as well as fail to hear

God's voice in them. Yet here is a most precious thing, that if the communion between a man and God is normal he may not be influenced by environment while at the same time he may allow that environment to speak to him. But if that man has offended the Lord and is thus out of fellowship, he may be affected by even the smallest incident and on the other hand not be able to hear any word from the biggest occurrence.

Hence here is a principle which is now placed before us, and we may test ourselves by it. If we are affected by environment and fail to hear its voice, we are proven to have lost contact with the Lord and to have fallen away. No circumstances should influence us, though they ought to speak to us.

We do not believe that there can be any environment into which we are placed without there being some word in it for us. We are fully convinced that in every circumstance God has something to say to us. There is hidden in the environment God's word to us. Naturally the "us" here points to each one of us individually. We sincerely believe that every daily occurrence speaks to each Christian.

If we live in the light of God we will come to see that for the sake of His way on earth as well as for the sake of His desire to possess us, God will arrange all things which should come to us. We ought not see only the appearance of things; we should know the Lord's ordering within the veil. What sweet feeling there will be in us if we can recognize what the Lord has arranged in the environment. Though we cannot say that all the circumstances are initiated by the throne, nevertheless we do affirm that all of them are governed by it. We believe there is a throne in heaven, and that our Lord, after His resurrection and ascension, does now sit on that throne—with all things having been put under His feet. So that God does indeed use the environment He has ordered to speak to His children. We therefore ought to receive words through our circumstances.

Two

Let us review the story of Jacob. Everybody agrees that the deepest experience of Jacob's life happened at the time he wrestled with God at Peniel. As a result of his wrestling, his name was changed. Even after he had such a deep experience at Peniel, God still raised up circumstances by which to speak to him. As recorded in Genesis 34, Jacob's daughter was humbled and his sons did much mischief. Jacob was under such environment that God spoke to him as shown in Genesis 35.

Some people may object by saying that at the time of Genesis 35 God spoke directly to Jacob, not speaking indirectly through environment. Not so, for if you read Genesis 34, you will see that God first put Jacob in the environment of Genesis 34 before He spoke to Jacob the words to be found in Genesis 35. What did God say to Jacob at this time? "Arise, go up to Bethel and dwell there: and make there an altar unto God, who appeared unto thee when thou fleddest from the face of Esau thy brother" (v.1). What story did God remind Jacob of? It was an old story, something which happened many years before. Because his brother Esau wanted to kill him, Jacob fled to his uncle on his mother's side. On his way he came to Bethel, where, because the sun had gone down, he passed the night. Jacob laid his head on a stone and fell asleep; whereupon God appeared to him in a dream. When he woke up, he vowed a vow, saying: "If God will be with me, and will keep me in this way that I go, and will give me bread to eat, and raiment to put on, so that I come again to my father's house in peace, and Jehovah will be my God, then this stone, which I have set up for a pillar, shall be God's house: and of all that thou shalt give me I will surely give the tenth unto thee" (Gen. 28.20–22). He made a vow before God.

Now is it not true that you vowed a vow when you were just saved? Although you may have *bargained* with God while making the vow, just as Jacob did, your heart was nonetheless right. As you commenced your walk along His path, your desire towards God was good. So that Jacob's condition is really a picture of our own condition. That morning after Jacob made his vow, he cast it behind his back. As he traveled eastward, he maneuvered this way and that so as to protect himself. Though he had asked God to keep him on his way and to clothe and feed him, yet he depended wholly on his own self. How perfectly he represents us! He looked to God, but he used his own cleverness. Nevertheless, after he had passed through all things, Jacob could only bow his head low and confess that all was God's mercy. Had it depended on him, he would have been no match for Laban. Jacob was tricky, but God prepared for him a Laban who was even more tricky. After he had been dealt with for twenty years, he was taken out of Laban's hand by the Lord. Jacob acknowledged that it was God's care for him.

Yet he forgot the vow which he earlier had made to God. For after he came back from Paddan-aram, he settled down at Shechem. Now we would no doubt think that after Jacob had received so much dealing, had passed through so much experience, suffered so very much, and accumulated such a large amount of possessions, that thereafter he could dwell at Shechem peacefully. But no, the God whom he served did not let him live on peacefully. Jacob's heart was satisfied, but not God's heart. What Jacob had wanted, God had given him; but what God had desired, Jacob had not yet given to Him. God must therefore continue to speak to him, and God did so again by environment. God knew that unless He gave Jacob a blow through environment, He would not be able to make him listen to His word.

Brothers and sisters, never consider yourselves so deeply spiritual that you need only to listen to the inner voice. No, many times God still has to speak to you through environment. No matter how great or small, heavy or light are your happenings, God has raised up these circumstances for Him to speak to you. We do not believe that a person can become so spiritual as to have no further need for environment to speak to him. In the life of every believer God must create a certain environment for him in order that He may say something to him.

You may have noticed that after Peniel Jacob had become quite spiritual, since he now was no longer Jacob but was Israel. After having gone through so much trial and dealing, he was irretrievably touched by God on that occasion. Jacob had become quite spiritual, and yet the Lord deemed it necessary to raise up another environment in order to speak to him. Jacob was thinking of settling down peacefully in Shechem, but God did not approve. The Bible leaves no record as to whether or not Jacob knew it inwardly. He might have sensed it somewhat, though such feeling may have passed quickly away. He paid no attention to his inward feeling if indeed he had had any. Yet we definitely know this, that God raised up an environment so that He might speak once again to Jacob. And what were the circumstances of this new environment? His daughter was humiliated, and his sons committed a gross crime—and these took away Jacob's peace.

At the time Jacob encountered such an environment, he had no thought that God was trying to speak to him through it; instead, he blamed his sons and became frightened. At this juncture God spoke to Jacob, saying: "Arise, go up to Bethel, and dwell there: and make there an altar unto God, who appeared unto thee when thou fleddest from the face of Esau thy brother." Let us understand from this, that the environment which Jacob met up with here actually prepared him to hear God's word. Without such circumstances he might have surmised that he now had everything and could thus pass his remaining days in peace. But the Lord raised up an environment which gave him no peace. So that what God meant by it was this: "All that you had asked of Me at the beginning, Jacob, I have given to you; but now you should fulfill the vow which you yourself had made to Me before." And hence God raised up this environment, and through it God spoke to Jacob. And when Jacob heard His voice, he once again brought himself and his household to the Lord and asked the Lord for cleansing.

Three

When the Lord touched Jacob this time, what came out of him? Ah, we witness the fact that all the foreign gods in his household came out. How incredible! That the man who knew God so well and had become so spiritual had not only forgotten his previous vows but still had many gods in his household as well. How often the idols which we hide will not come out at the beckoning of the inner voice but will only come out when pressed by outward environment. Beloved, in order to return to Bethel, these things must be handed over! Oh, if we are careless about our original heart wish and permit unlawful things to remain in our lives—and regardless of our protestations that we will be led inwardly and will listen to the inner voice—God will raise up an environment to hit us so as to strike down the foreign gods in our lives. God will not only ferret out the golden rings but also many other illegitimate matters.

Oftentimes in our fellowship with the Lord we sense no condemnation and do not feel much wrong; yet when God raises up a certain environment to touch us, we will discover some hidden idols which we were unwilling to give up. We dare not be so confident of ourselves as to conclude that we are all right if we feel peace within. Yes indeed, we *should* turn within to hear the inner voice. Nevertheless, we ought also to realize how deep is our fall—how difficult it is for us to stand and yet how easy to fall. Consequently, many times our inner feeling is not keen enough and our inward reproof is not sharp enough. We still need to let God speak to us through environment.

We may have been a Christian for many years. According to our experience we may have advanced very far from "our" first time in Bethel. But according to our heart desire we may have lost the desire of consecration which we initially made at

Bethel. God longs to see us having more experiences; but how He also delights to see that we keep the first heart desire afresh. Brethren, no matter how experienced we are, we need to return to Bethel. Look again at Jacob. How much of God truly had been incorporated and increased in him through his many experiences, yet he lost the desire of consecration which he had first made at Bethel. Accordingly, God raised up an environment by which He could speak to him. A spiritual person such as Jacob still had need of an environment for God to be able to speak to him.

Please realize that the inner voice alone is not enough; sometimes there is a need for some outside environment to speak forth God's word. You would like to live peacefully at Shechem, but God will raise up some circumstance to make it uncomfortable for you to remain that way. He wants you to perform your original heart desire of consecration; He wants you to go back to Bethel. You have forgotten your heart desire, but God has not forgotten. You no longer maintain your consecration, but God still desires you to do so. And hence the environment.

Consecration is great in revealing personal fault. Each time you return to your first heart desire you will see in your life things that have become irrelevant or places where you have fallen. Yes, every time you come back to Bethel you will discover in yourself so many things you should no longer harbor and so many areas wherein you have truly fallen. Consequently, never consider yourself so spiritual as to have no further problem. Instead, go and pray. Pray like this: "O Lord, seven years ago when I was spiritually revived, I prayed one night that I wanted to consecrate and lay everything on the altar for You. And today I still give all things to You." As you return to your first heart desire you will know how many things in your life are no longer relevant and how far you have fallen away from your first heart desire.

It is true that you are much more experienced than before, and you may even boast in this fact, saying, "I know more of God than before, and I am more experienced too." But when you return to your first desire, you will discover that, though you are now more experienced, you nonetheless have fallen, in that you still have idols and golden earrings. There are many things which should be buried. You must first bury these idols and golden earrings under the oak at Shechem before you can return to Bethel to serve God. From this incident we can see how experienced Jacob was, and yet how he did not go back to Bethel until God had spoken to him through environment.

Let us therefore inquire as to whether there is indeed the voice of God in our environment which calls us to return to Bethel. You may have reached a place wherein you have everything you need and simply wish to settle down in peace. Will God allow you to stay on peacefully this way? You have found rest, but does God find rest? Have you satisfied Him with the heart desire of Bethel? A great number of brothers and sisters need the Lord to use environment to call them back to Bethel, that is, to cause them to return to their first heart desire. In case you have lost that first heart desire, God will surely arrange some circumstances by which to stir you, discomfort you, and make you hear His word in you. We do not believe that the environment He has arranged will only outwardly affect us without giving us any word. Even with such a spiritual man as Jacob, God still needed to raise up some environment through which to put into Jacob His word.

Hence do not assume that as long as you are peaceful in heart you are all right. Sometimes your feelings may deceive you. You say you are peaceful in heart, but have you received more corrections from the Lord during these days? Are you being increasingly awakened? How much do you allow the Lord to possess you? How much have you been stripped by Him? Just remember that there ought to be the Lord's word to you in environment. We should hear the voice of God through circumstance, go back to Bethel, and return to the first heart desire of consecration so that God may be satisfied.

5 Numbering Our Days

So teach us to number our days, that we may get us a heart of wisdom. (Ps. 90.12)

Redeeming the time, because the days are evil. Wherefore be ye not foolish, but understand what the will of the Lord is. (Eph. 5.16,17)

And I will restore to you the years that the locust hath eaten, the canker-worm, and the caterpillar, and the palmer-worm, my great army which I sent among you. (Joel 2.25)

As recorded in the Psalms, Moses had prayed to God, saying, "So teach us to number our days, that we may get us a heart of wisdom." In counting according to the calendar, the days we have spent can easily be tallied up, since a day is a day and a year is a year. But in counting according to God, some days are accredited whereas other days are rejected. Because our days on earth are limited, we need to learn how we can number them so as to please God and to have every day and every year sanctioned by Him. Such is the problem on which we will now focus our attention.

One

In Genesis 4 and 5 we are presented with two genealogies. In Chapter 4 is the genealogy of Cain; in Chapter 5, that of Seth. The methods of recording these two genealogies are quite different. That of Cain is very brief: there is no recounting the age of Cain and of his descendants. The genealogy of Seth, however, is more detailed: a certain person is shown to have lived to a specific age and to have begotten a certain other person, and then to have lived on for a specific period of years before finally dying. Generation after generation, these years are recorded in great detail. From these two genealogies—one brief and one full—we may discover on what basis God numbers our days. The reason for Cain's genealogy being so brief is because he sinned against God and was far away from God, having had no fellowship with Him. On the other hand, Seth's genealogy is full because he had succeeded Abel and had communed with God and God was pleased with him. It can therefore be said that our spiritual days are counted according to our particular condition before God. When we were far away from Him, being dead in sins and trangressions, our days were not numbered before God. Our spiritual days only commence with our repentance and our turning to the Lord as we begin to fellowship with Him.

When the children of Israel came out of Egypt God commanded them, saying, "This month shall be unto you the beginning of months: it shall be the first month of the year to you" (Ex. 12.2). The first month of the year is the year's beginning, and hence the starting point for numbering days. During this month the children of Israel had slain the paschal lamb, had come out of Egypt, and been delivered from the hand of Pharaoh. Whereupon God had designated this particular month to be the beginning of their year. Thereafter they were to have a new beginning before the Lord.

Let me ask you, How long is your spiritual age? Someone may be 50 or 60 years old physically, yet his spiritual age may be only a year, or even a month. One's spiritual year is counted only from the day one is born again. The day you receive the salvation of the Lord is the day you begin your spiritual history. Before that moment you really have no spiritual days to be so accredited in the sight of God. Furthermore, even after you have believed the Lord, it is not certain that each day or year necessarily counts thereafter. You may have already believed the Lord for five whole years, yet you may not be a five-year-old Christian before God. That is to say, some of the days subsequent to your having become a Christian are not numbered. In the Bible we can notice that such days are ignored and unrecorded, because God has looked upon them as wasted days, and therefore not credited.

Two

Let us see how many years there were from the time of the exodus to the beginning of the building of the temple by Solomon.

> And for about the time of forty years as a nursing-father bare he them in the wilderness. And when he had destroyed seven nations in the land of Canaan, he gave them their land for an inheritance, for about four hundred and fifty years: and after these things he gave them judges until Samuel the prophet. And afterward they asked for a king: and God gave unto them Saul the son of Kish, a man of the tribe of Benjamin, for the space of forty years. And when he had removed him, he raised up David to be their king . . . (Acts 13.18–22a)

Now David had been king for 40 years (see 2 Sam. 5.4). So how many years were there from the exodus to the fourth year of the reign of Solomon when he began to build the temple? Forty years plus 450 years equal 490 years; adding to it 40 years two times will bring the number to 570 years; adding further the three years of Solomon's reign before he commenced building the temple, the total reaches 573 years. Yet in 1 Kings it says: "And it came to pass in the four hundred and eightieth year after the children of Israel were come out of the land of Egypt, in the fourth year of Solomon's reign over Israel, in the month Ziv, which is the second month, that he began to build the house of Jehovah" (6.1). Here we are told of 480 years, not 573—a difference of 93 years!

Why is there such a discrepancy? Is the record of the book of Acts incorrect, or even that of 1 Kings? No, neither record is wrong. In the difference of years between these two records lies a very important spiritual principle. By comparing the records of Acts with those in the Old Testament, we find that the 40 years in the wilderness, Saul's 40 years, David's 40 years, and Solomon's three years before he commenced the building of the temple are all unquestionably correct. The only figure open to question is the 450 years. In that period 1 Kings numbers 93 years less than Acts. How can we account for these apparently missing 93 years? In searching the book of Judges we discover the following fact, that during those years the children of Israel had been oppressed by foreign nations on several occasions. Accordingly, let us see from Judges how many years were due to such oppression.

"Therefore the anger of Jehovah was kindled against Israel, and he sold them into the hand of Cu-shan-rish-a-tha-im king of Mesopotamia: and the children of Israel served Cu-shan-rish-a-tha-im eight years" (Judges 3.8). This was Israel's first oppression, which lasted for eight years. "And the children of Israel served Eglon the king of Moab eighteen years" (3.14). This was Israel's second oppression, which spanned 18 years. "And Jehovah sold them into the hand of Jabin king of Canaan, that reigned in Hazor; the captain of whose host was Sisera, who dwelt in Harosheth of the Gentiles. And the children of Israel cried unto Jehovah: for he had nine hundred chariots of iron; and twenty years he mightily oppressed the children of Israel" (4.2,3). This was Israel's third oppression, which was prolonged for 20 years. "And the children of Israel did that which was evil in the sight of Jehovah: and Jehovah delivered them into the hand of Midian seven years" (6.1). Here was Israel's fourth oppression, and its duration was seven years. "And the children of Israel again did that which was evil in the sight of Jehovah; and Jehovah delivered them into the hand of the Philistines forty years" (13.1). This was Israel's fifth oppression, in which they served the Philistines for 40 years.

How many years, therefore, was Israel oppressed by foreign countries these five times? Eight years plus 18 years plus 20 years plus seven years plus 40 years come to 93 years, no more and no less. And thus we have found the solution. In Acts Paul was narrating a *history* of the Israelites; hence he included these 93 years. 1 Kings, however, emphasized the *condition* of the children of Israel before God, and therefore excluded these 93 years.

The fact of these 93 years not being numbered is very meaningful. These were lost years, for whenever the children of Israel lost their freedom and thus served the Gentiles and were without a judge of their own, their years were not counted at all. They were a people who had been delivered out of Egypt and who belonged to God. But when subsequently they were ruled by their enemies— being enslaved and under bondage once again— they could not freely serve God. And hence these days were never numbered: such days that they served anyone other than God were automatically considered lost, and consequently the Lord did not number them.

Just here we should pause and consider how many days from the time we were saved onward have actually been accredited by God. You may have believed the Lord for eight or ten years, yet how many of these days have in reality been spent foolishly? What discount has had to be made on our past days? Oh, we have wasted too much time! We would probably have to wonder whether, of these many years, a sufficient number of days could ever add up to *just one* accountable year before God! We should realize that the days which we live according to our own human will, away from God, defeated and fallen, will not be numbered by Him. Let us ask ourselves honestly: I have been a Christian for a number of years, but how many days of these years have been wasted,

and how many days have been numbered by God?
Let us truly see that all the days of our having lost
communion with God are uncredited. None, therefore, can afford not to redeem the time.

Three

Do not fancy that the lost days will not amount
to much, since apparently they are merely some
scattered days. For if we were simply to look at the
wilderness journey taken by the children of Israel,
we would be shown how serious are the wasted
days indeed. In the third month after they had
come out of Egypt they arrived at Mount Sinai (see
Ex. 19.1). They remained at Sinai for ten months,
but on the twentieth day of the second month of
the second year after the exodus they left Sinai and
journeyed towards the land God had promised
them as their inheritance (see Num. 10.11,12). Now
it is recorded that it was an "eleven days' journey
from Horeb by the way of Mount Seir unto
Kadesh-barnea" (Deut. 1.2). Please note that Kadesh-barnea was at the border of the land of
Canaan. So that upon their leaving Mount Sinai
the children of Israel could have entered Canaan
immediately after an eleven days' journey. Yet
because of their unbelief they did not enter Canaan
after their arrival at Kadesh-barnea, but instead
wandered in the wilderness for 38 years before
their descendants did finally enter the Promised
Land. What a circle they had traveled! Not three

or five years, but 38 long years. Originally they could have entered the Promised Land within a two year period after Egypt; now, though, they had had to spend 38 more years.

Oh how many are the days we have wasted in our spiritual journey! Whereas a problem could have been solved in three or five days, in the case of some people it remains unsolved even after three to five years. Such a situation is not unlike that of the children of Israel who circled around and around in the wilderness wasting many years. Such a loss is truly great, and ought never to be viewed as insignificant.

Four

In the life of Abraham we can clearly see how many of his days were numbered and how many were not. According to the word of Acts 7.2–3, while Abraham was in Ur of Mesopotamia, God appeared to him, saying: "Get thee out of thy land, and from thy kindred, and come into the land that I shall show thee." And how did Abraham respond? Had he not listened to God at all he would have felt uneasy inside; yet to follow God absolutely, this he was reluctant to do. Hence he only obeyed halfway. God had told Abraham to leave his kindred behind, but he took his kindred with him: he took his nephew Lot, and his father Terah also went along. Moreover, God's thought was for Abraham to go all the way to Canaan, but he settled down at Haran instead (see Gen. 11.31). Such an attitude is a perfect picture of the condition of a double-minded Christian. Abraham was like that. Yes, he came out of Ur of Chaldea, but he stopped far short of entering Canaan. He was like a halfway Christian.

After the death of Abraham's father Terah, God called Abraham again (see Gen. 12.1). This time He called him at Haran. The Lord's purpose never wavers. Once He decides upon something, He will certainly accomplish it. Since God wanted Abraham to go to Canaan, He would not change His mind even if Abraham lingered at Haran. At God's first call, Abraham obeyed only halfway. So He called him the second time. Now it is recorded in the Bible that when Abraham obeyed God and left Haran, he was 75 years old at the time (see Gen. 12.4). Please note that there was no record of his age while he was in Ur, nor was there any record of his age when he was in Haran. It was only at the moment when he came out of Haran to go to Canaan that his being 75 years old was pointed out. This, I believe, indicates to us the beginning of a new recognition of his days. Abraham's days in Haran, constituting as they did a stopping midway in God's purpose, were lost days; therefore, they were not recorded.

As we look back on our own past history, how many days have been lost! We need to learn from the life of Abraham that all days at places like Haran are ignored by God. Oftentimes we walk after our own will and seek for ease and comfort. We stop and stay at midway. These are days at Haran and will not be reckoned. To be blessed of God, we, like Abraham, must come out of Haran. When Abraham was 75, in that year he left Haran. The Bible records it, for God deems it worthy to be recounted. It reveals how He desires man's absolute obedience.

Yet Abraham did not lose some days just this one time. He suffered loss also in the matter of having seed. God had promised him a son; nevertheless, he took his handmaid Hagar as concubine on the recommendation of his wife. Abraham committed a presumptuous sin before the Lord. Subsequently, Hagar bore a son. But this son was born through Abraham's fleshly strength, not through the promise of God. Accordingly, we find at the end of Genesis chapter 16 that the age of Abraham is given as 86 years and at the beginning of chapter 17 his age is given as 99 years. Thirteen years are missing in the record. During these 13 years, nothing is recorded concerning him. No altar was built by him, neither did God appear to him nor give him any new revelation or promise. These were blank days, as though they never existed. During those days, Ishmael grew up. Hence this period of years in Abraham's life was wasted and lost.

Brothers and sisters, during the years that are upon you, are you having new experiences, new lights and new words from the Lord? Is there anybody being delivered through your instrumentality? Is there anyone being helped by you? Are you having a deeper knowledge of God? Are you receiving new assurances concerning God's promises? Are you experiencing a renewed consecration before Him? If you are not experiencing such things as these, then these days of yours are lost days. They are wasted days. An elderly sister once said that "the way to reward for a Christian is to make every day count." How pitiful that sometimes in our Christian walk ten days are expended without their adding up to even one real day! Let us instead be Christians diligently day by day. If we spend our days foolishly—that is, if we rebel against God, commit sins, or walk after our own will—our days will be totally wasted so far as God is concerned. And how dreadful that is.

Why, though, did the Bible record Abraham's 99 years of age? Because in that year he received the rite of circumcision and a year later he begat Isaac. The meaning of circumcision is to cut off the flesh. If we walk in the flesh, our days are wasted. May we instead cast aside all that is of the flesh and offer ourselves wholly on the altar that we may no longer waste our days. Let us not lose 49 years out of our 50. Let us note how many days have been foolishly spent and how many days are still left. Were we to wait daily for the Lord's coming, we would be careful in our daily life.

Five

The Lord spoke a parable, as told in Matthew 20, about a man going out several times to find laborers for his vineyard. Let us notice especially these two words in the parable: "standing idle". The householder "went out about the third hour, and saw others standing in the marketplace idle; and to them he said, Go ye also into the vineyard" (v.3,4a). "And about the eleventh hour he went out, and found others standing; and he saith unto them, Why stand ye here all the day idle? . . . Go ye also into the vineyard" (v.6,7). This parable tells us that God does not want us to stand idle but to work. It also tells us that God has His determined field of labor—the vineyard. Perhaps you will say you are very busy and have no leisure. But *where* on earth are you so busy? If you are not working in the vineyard, what difference is that from "standing idle"? If you are not living in the will of God, you are in God's sight as one standing idle, no matter how much other work you have been doing. Or possibly you are busily engaged in so-called spiritual work, yet God may still say to you: "Why do you stand idle? Works done outside of *this* vineyard are not Mine." Though you may be very busy, in God's eye you are idle nonetheless. Only works done *in the vineyard* are recognized by Him. Such works originate in God and are for God. If your work is done outside His will, all the days you have spent on it are reckoned by Him as making you as one who is standing idle.

The word of the householder to those who stood idle at the eleventh hour was: "Why stand ye here all the day idle?" "All the day" points to a lifetime. How about you? Are you standing all the day idle? Or are you working in the vineyard? Do not misunderstand me as suggesting that you should resign from your work and preach. What is most essential is that whatever we do we must be clear we are standing in the will of God. Working in the vineyard means working in the will of God. And in the vineyard of His will are all sorts of labors: some laborers are digging the ground, some are sowing the seed, and some are making repairs. No matter what work is being done, it will be acceptable if it is done for the good of the vineyard. And hence we need not be so exclusive as to consider only certain walks or works done by certain people as being God's works. No, as long as the days are spent *in the vineyard*, they will be remembered.

You may have been saved for three or five years, or even ten or 20 years. Yet how much of your time has been spent for God? Doubtless you have done a lot, but for whom do you work? All is well if you know with certainty that you do the will of God. God has not required every Christian to lay down his job and preach the gospel full-time. And some who *are* doing full-time gospel work may not be in His will at all. The question therefore is this: what is your heart attitude towards God's will? This makes consecration absolutely necessary. If you have had only a little heart for God since being saved, your life is deemed as being nothing but a standing idle.

Six

"And I, brethren, could not speak unto you as unto spiritual, but as unto carnal, as unto babes in Christ. I fed you with milk, not with meat; for ye were not yet able to bear it: nay, not even now are ye able" (1 Cor. 3.1,2). Paul wrote this to the saints at Corinth. So far as we know only a few years had passed by between the first time Paul had preached at Corinth and the time he wrote this first letter to the Corinthian believers. And even by then Paul already felt that the saints at Corinth had not grown properly. Even though they had been Christians for only a few years, nevertheless he did not exonerate them from any blame of being childish. On the contrary, he chided them for casting away many days, because they ought to have grown and yet they had not. In Paul's opinion these relatively young believers should now be strong and capable of eating meat, but they had wasted so many days that they remained as carnal babies. They should be well experienced in the way of the Lord—both in obeying and in trusting the Lord—so as to be teachers to others, yet they were as ignorant now as they had been before. True, they were Christians for just a few years, but Paul felt strongly that they should not remain as babes.

Here is something for us to take to heart. If we think we can remain babies because we have not been saved for too many years, we are gravely mistaken. How many are the days of our life as a Christian? Should it be that we have believed the Lord for eight or ten years but are no different from the time when we were first born again, that is to say, if we are still carnal, we have most certainly wasted many of our days.

How many days can be lived on earth? Normally, only 70 or 80 years. How short, then, *are* our days! How many days are left after deducting the days during which we were unsaved? And do any of us know how much longer we will live on earth? Suppose a person is already 60; perhaps God will say to him: "You have not lived ten years before Me." Or a person may be 40; and perhaps God will say: "You have not lived even a few days before Me." How pitiful it is that so many days are lost.

Seven

I know that our hearts ache over the years we have foolishly wasted. But thank God, He gives us comfort; for He tells us through the book of Joel: "I will restore to you the years that the locust hath eaten, the canker-worm, and the caterpillar, and the palmer-worm, my great army which I sent among you" (2.25). Thank God, He still has a way. Maybe you are now 60, and you have wasted 30 or 40 of your years. You will lament: "Alas, the opportunity is gone. My best years have been eaten up by locusts. The lost years can never be regained now. What shall I do?" Praise God, He will restore to us these years that the locusts have eaten. As to the days wasted, ten years may have been counted as only one day. But if we hereafter redeem the time, one day may become equal to a thousand days—"for a day in thy courts, is better than a thousand," said David (Ps. 84.10). The day on earth is not clocked in heaven on the basis of 24 hours. God has instead His special way of computation. If our service is according to His will, one day in His sight may be reckoned as many days.

Once there was a young man who fell into sin and was dying of tuberculosis. An elderly servant of God preached the gospel to him, telling him how the Lord Jesus had borne all his sins, and urging him to repent, confess his sins and receive the Lord Jesus to be his Savior. At first this youth felt quite reluctant, being obsessed with the thought of how ever could the Lord forgive such a sinner as he. Yet finally he did accept the Lord and was saved. He felt so happy and peaceful. After a few days the elderly servant of God revisited him, finding his face full of grief and pain. So he asked the young believer: "Why are you so sad? Do not let Satan deceive you!" He answered: "I know my sins have been forgiven." "Then why are you so sad?" Forlornly he answered: "My days on earth are quite finished. What can I bring to the Lord when I shall stand before Him? My hands are empty.

Must I go and see the Lord empty-handed?" Such was the reason for his grief. In answer, the elderly man comforted him by saying: "Brother, do not be discouraged. I will use your word to write a song. And whoever is constrained by this song to go abroad to preach the gospel and win souls, you shall have the reward." Now this was the song that Charles C. Luther wrote which has since become famous: "Must I go and empty-handed? Must I meet my Savior so?" Many have been aroused by this song and have fervently served the Lord. Although this young man had lost many of his days, he still retained a little heart desire for the Lord at his dying, and the Lord fulfilled it.

May we all remember our days! May our lost days be restored. May each day be equal to a thousand days. And may we step by step walk in the light of God's will!

6

The Lord Is Never Discouraged

Jesus answered and said unto her, Every one that drinketh of this water shall thirst again; but whosoever drinketh of the water that I shall give him shall never thirst; but the water that I shall give him shall become in him a well of water springing up unto eternal life. (John 4.13,14)

Now when he was in Jerusalem at the passover, during the feast, many believed on his name, beholding his signs which he did. But Jesus did not trust himself unto them, for that he knew all men. (2.23,24)

Jesus therefore perceiving that they were about to come and take him by force, to make him king, withdrew again into the mountain himself alone. (6.15)

His brethren therefore said unto him, Depart hence, and go into Judea, that thy disciples also may behold thy works which thou doest. For no man doeth any-

thing in secret, and himself seeketh to be known openly.
. . . Jesus therefore saith unto them, My time is not yet
come; but your time is always ready. . . . And having
said these things unto them, he abode still in Galilee.
(7.3,4,6,9)

Verily, verily, I say unto you, Except a grain of
wheat fall into the earth and die, it abideth by itself
alone; but if it die, it beareth much fruit. (12.24)

Peter saith unto him, Lord, why cannot I follow thee
even now? I will lay down my life for thee. Jesus
answereth, Wilt thou lay down thy life for me? Verily,
verily, I say unto thee, The cock shall not crow, till thou
hast denied me thrice. (13.37,38)

Jesus answered them, Do ye now believe? Behold,
the hour cometh, yea, is come, that ye shall be scattered,
every man to his own, and shall leave me alone: and yet
I am not alone, because the Father is with me. These
things have I spoken unto you, that in me ye may have
peace. In the world ye have tribulation: but be of good
cheer; I have overcome the world. (16.31–33)

Nothing that our Lord has done on earth fails
to be good. The Gospel according to Mark has this
word to say: "He hath done all things well" (7.37).
Whatever He does is indeed good. We would now
like to talk about what the Lord Jesus has in fact
done, and directing special attention to the words
found in John 4.13,14.

There the Lord Jesus says how He will fill the
heart of the Christians so that they will no longer
be unsatisfied. He himself has promised us this:

that "every one that drinketh of this water shall thirst again: but whosoever drinketh of the water that I shall give him shall never thirst." Anyone who drinks of the water which the Lord gives will have his thirst forever quenched, and thus he will never sense any lack nor will he ever be disappointed. We will naturally ask the question, though, whether this really is so. Our answer is: Yes, it *is* so. We who have received the Lord Jesus may truly never be thirsty again. But why is it, then, that some people nevertheless feel unsatisfied? For there are some who will continue to say: I am still thirsty; I have yet to attain some things. Is this because the promise of the Lord is not fulfilled? Not at all, for He clearly announces that "whosoever drinketh of the water that I shall give him shall never thirst." The Lord gives *permanent* satisfaction to people.

Why, then, are some of us still thirsty? Why are we unsatisfied? Why is there yet a desiring within us? Why is there pining? Why are we yet sorrowful? And why is there still self-pity? This is because we are attentive only to the promise in verse 14 but forget to see the declaration of verse 13. The Lord does indeed say here that "whosoever drinketh of the water that I shall give him shall never thirst"; but please note that He first declares this: that "every one that drinketh of this water shall thirst again"—that is to say, "this water" refers to the water of this world, the water which Jacob left behind, the best of the water of this world.

Many people do not comprehend the true nature of the water of this world. They are ignorant of the properties inherent in what the world is able to offer them: whether they are temporary or permanent, visible or invisible, material or spiritual. Consequently, they do not realize that in order to obtain the Lord's promise of satisfying their heart, they must first understand how the water of this world cannot satisfy them. First know this, that "every one that drinketh of this water shall thirst again"; but then comprehend what the Lord says next, that a person "shall never thirst." The Lord intends to satisfy us fully, so that we need not hope for one thing after we have gotten something else, resulting in our never being satisfied.

Here we will not dwell on how the water of this world cannot satisfy man's heart; rather, we will focus on explaining why so many Christians still feel thirsty today. The reason for such a phenomenon is found in the fact of their returning again and again to drink of the water mentioned in verse 13. Why is a person disappointed? If there is never any expectation, there will never be disappointment. If a man never expects to be rich, he will never be disappointed because of having no wealth. On the other hand, if we expect the water of this world to satisfy us—that is to say, if our eyes are turned in the wrong direction—we will be thirsty again. Here is the explanation, I believe, for why so many of us feel hurt and are disappointed.

Why are we not satisfied? There is a reason. It

is simply because we look for these transient things to satisfy our desires. Yet we will never be satisfied if we seek for such passing things as fame and wealth. For when we get them in our hands, we will discover that they do not comfort us, neither gladden nor satisfy us. And immediately we will long for something else. And thus we will thirst and thirst and thirst again. Hence our mistake is in expecting these fleeting things to fill our hearts. As we grasp after these things we will see how soon they shall pass away; so that our heart can never really be satisfied.

The Lord Is Never Discouraged

Our Lord Jesus Christ is never discouraged. In our consideration together on this point, let us concentrate on what the Gospel according to John has to say about Him (the other three Gospels, of course, have much to say about the Lord also). Judging by the things which happened in His life—the circumstances He faced throughout His earthly walk—the Lord Jesus could have been discouraged or been in despair many times. Yet, He never was. Isaiah 49 alludes to Him, it there stating that God will use Him to bring Jacob back again and to re-gather Israel. But what is the apparent result? We know that by all outward appearances it seems like a total failure. How about the Lord's own feeling, as recorded in the same chapter of Isaiah? "I have labored in vain,"

He says; "I have spent my strength for nought and vanity; yet surely the justice due to me is with Jehovah, and my recompense with my God" (v.4). He is never discouraged. Isaiah 42 also makes reference to the Lord: "He will not fail nor be discouraged" (v.4). Though the things which happen to Him could so easily and naturally cause fainting and despair, nonetheless He is never discouraged.

Turning to the New Testament, we find that there is a difference in emphasis between the Gospel of John and the Gospel of Matthew. In John's Gospel the Lord is rejected by men from the very outset, whereas in Matthew He is shown as not being rejected until after Chapter 12. In the very first chapter of John it is recorded that the Lord "came unto his own, and they that were his own received him not" (v.11). He came to bear the sins of the children of Israel as well as the sins of the Gentiles. But men rejected Him and would not accept Him. While the Lord was on the cross He was rejected by men and even forsaken by God.

Were *we* ever put into such a situation, we doubtless would be disappointed, discouraged, and extremely hurt. Yet on the cross the Lord cried aloud: "It is finished"! (John 19.30) Had *we* been there in His place we would have cried out: "Licked!"; but He shouted, as would a victorious army, "It is done!" Throughout His life He took God as His satisfaction. He never put any hope in men, nor did He expect anything from men. His expectation lay solely in God. For God was His recompense. The Lord himself declared that no one knew the Son but the Father and that He never received glory from men. Moreover, He said that He came not to do His own will but to do the will of Him who had sent Him. He announced how He always did the will of the Father. All through His life our Lord took the Father's will as His satisfaction. His satisfaction was found in God and God alone. Hence for this reason, no matter how changeable were the people and things and events of the world about Him, nothing could discourage Him. Whoever therefore makes God his satisfaction shall never be disappointed.

Negatively speaking, let us understand that we should never hope in men. If we do not expect fame, glory, help, comfort, sustenance, and so forth from men, we will never be thirsty. Oh let us be careful about our attitude towards the water of this world. For the way we look at the world will surely determine what we expect of the world.

The Lord Seeks No Glory from Men

"Now when he was in Jerusalem at the passover, during the feast, many believed on his name, beholding his signs which he did. But Jesus *did not trust himself unto them,* for that he knew all men" (John 2.23,24).

We note in the second chapter of John that the Lord performed two great miracles. After He had performed the first one, His disciples believed in Him. And with the working of the second miracle, many more saw the signs which He did and believed on His name. From our point of view, if we notice that the number of people attending our meetings are increasing and that those believing in the gospel we preach also are multiplying, our heart will unconsciously become entrapped by the work. Not so with the Lord, though. For take note of verse 24: "But Jesus did not trust himself unto them, for that he knew all men." He refused to take enjoyment in men, nor would He at all trust Himself to them, because He knew that many of these very same people would crucify Him later on. No doubt, the Lord rejoiced when many believed on Him; even so, He would not commit Himself to them. It was not a matter of His not allowing these people to touch His heart; rather, it showed how the work never swayed His heart, regardless its success. As a consequence, He was able to maintain His objectivity.

"I receive not glory from men" (John 5.41). Here is recorded the story of a man who, sick with an incurable disease for 38 years, was healed instantaneously by the Lord. Many who had formerly opposed Him no longer did so. Instead they glorified God. Yet the Lord Jesus said: "I do not receive glory from men." Now if the same situation were to happen to us, we would probably welcome glory from men. And should we indeed be those who expect men to give us glory, we will be glad if they give it to us but very disappointed if they do not. Our Lord, however, never received glory from men. He neither expected nor accepted anything from men, with the result that He was never disappointed.

"Jesus therefore perceiving that they were about to come and take him by force, to make him king, withdrew again into the mountain himself alone" (John 6.15). At that time several thousands were gathered together. And upon witnessing the sign of the distribution of the loaves, they acclaimed that this Man was their King. Although many highly exalted Him, the Lord refused their exaltation of Him. He would not receive any glory from them. What men would give Him, He would not accept. He would not drink of the water of this world. Because God in Him had already satisfied His heart, He could resist all that the world would give Him. So that His concrete reaction was to withdraw. To "withdraw" is the best attitude to have. Withdrawal can keep a servant of God from being damaged by the exaltation of men. By withdrawing, a person is given the opportunity to prove the satisfaction that comes from God. Withdrawing is due to the inward satisfaction that comes from God.

"His brethren therefore said unto him, Depart hence, and go into Judea, that thy disciples also may behold thy works which thou doest. For no man doeth anything in secret, and himself seeketh to be known openly. If thou doest these things, manifest thyself to the world. . . . Jesus therefore saith unto them, My time is not yet come; but your time is always ready. . . . And having said these things unto them, he abode still in Galilee" (John 7.3,4,6,9). At that moment the brethren of the Lord Jesus thought that He could become famous if He were to perform more signs. Hence they told the Lord that He should go to where the people were. For here in Galilee He was seen neither by His disciples nor by the Jews; how then could they ever believe on Him? Jerusalem, on the other hand, was a metropolis where large numbers of people congregated. There, He would become famous and be believed on by many. Nonetheless, Jesus "abode still in Galilee." Although it was fairly simple to move to another place, and by such a move there would be brought to Him numerous advantages, Jesus refused to do so.

In contrast to Jesus most other people are curious. And how many are the praises which spring from man's curiosity. If only the Lord were willing to change His lodging, He would have countless opportunities to be praised of men! Yet He did not trust himself to them. He rejected special praises from men. And why? Because He was so full inside that He needed nothing from the outside. Knowing the nature of the water of this world so well, the Lord could speak to the women —who bewailed and lamented Him while on the way to the cross—in this fashion: "Weep not for me, but weep for yourselves, and for your children" (Luke 23.28). He was neither disappointed nor ever discouraged.

"Verily, verily, I say unto you, Except a grain of wheat fall into the earth and die, it abideth by itself alone; but if it die, it beareth much fruit" (John 12.24). In this chapter of John's Gospel our Lord is seen as seemingly experiencing the most glorious day of His entire life. Not only His friends believed in Him, but many Jews believed in Him as well. Even the Pharisees spoke to one another on this wise: "Behold how ye prevail nothing; lo, the world is gone after him" (v.19). His enemies conceded defeat, His friends trusted in Him, and many Jews now believed on Him. Moreover, even some Gentiles came to Him. For it is recorded that certain Greeks drew near and asked Philip to tell the Lord Jesus that they would like to see Him. By their words or actions, then, all these people unanimously acknowledged that this was indeed a day of victory for the Lord Jesus.

Now were we to find ourselves in such a prosperous situation, we would most certainly lose our head. Yet how about the Lord Jesus? At that very moment He answered His disciples in this way: "Except a grain of wheat fall into the earth and die, it abideth by itself alone; but if it die, it beareth much fruit." And this, we are told, He spoke concerning His own death (see v.33). It seems as if the Lord was saying to Philip: the road which My Father has sent Me to travel along is not all the time riding upon an ass victoriously into

Jerusalem, nor is it always My being welcomed or cheered or sought after by men. The world might offer all that they had to Him, but He would neither enjoy it nor accept their offer. He refused to drink even a drop of the water of this world. He rejected that which men would give Him, because He desired only what God gave Him.

We should learn this lesson. The Lord's workers must especially take this to heart. For *today* people may turn their faces towards you, but *tomorrow* they may show you their heels. The multitude who in Jesus' time shouted "Hosanna" on that triumphant day were the very same people who cried out "Away with him" very shortly afterwards. Yet the Lord was not discouraged by their fickle actions. He possessed a secret resistance in Him against the favor of men. He never maintained any direct relationship with His environment. All that He cared for was God and the will of God. Hence, unlike man's way that is so clearly crooked, His way was always straight. Our Lord had never allowed His friends to bend His way: neither the praises of men nor the opposition of enemies could ever change His course.

"The Father Is with Me"

"Peter saith unto him, Lord, why cannot I follow thee even now? I will lay down my life for thee. Jesus answereth, Wilt thou lay down thy life for me? Verily, verily, I say unto thee, The cock

shall not crow, till thou hast denied me thrice"
(John 13.37,38). All the temptations thus far mentioned came either from the glory of men or from
the subtlety of the enemy. Now the Lord was faced
with an even more subtle trial given Him by Peter.
Peter remonstrated: "Why cannot I follow thee
even now? I will lay down my life for thee." The
Lord answered: "The cock shall not crow, till thou
hast denied me thrice."

It seems to me that Peter many times had
walked before the Lord and had helped the Lord,
but the Lord did not entrust himself even to Peter.
Now if I would ever have had disciples (but of
course I shall never have any) and a particular
disciple had helped me a lot in the past, I would no
doubt cast an evil eye towards him if he should
ever dare to deny me while I was being judged in
some court. With the glance of my eye towards him
I would mean to say to that disciple: "Do you dare
to deny me?" But not so in the case of our Lord
with Peter. He instead turned and looked at Peter
in such a way as to cause His disciple to go out and
to weep bitterly. In this connection there is a very
moving hymn which runs in part as follows:

> What has stripped the seeming beauty
>   From the idols of the earth?
> Not a sense of right or duty,
>   But the sight of peerless worth.

> 'Tis that look that melted Peter,

'Tis that face that Stephen saw,
'Tis that heart that wept with Mary,
    Can alone from idols draw.

If our Lord's two eyes should ever give us a look, it
alone would melt us completely.

Yet this look of the Lord's at Peter has about it
another revelation. We expect too much from *our*
disciple. So we become greatly disappointed and
deeply hurt when he fails us or speaks unworthily
of us. Unlike the Lord with *His* Peter, we cannot
stand the misunderstanding and unfaithfulness of
our Peter. In fact, though, if we drink of the water
of this world, expecting friends and relatives and
other people to satisfy us, we shall always be left
thirsty again. But if we were to rejoice only in what
God has provided—whether house, friends, food or
other things—we would be able to be satisfied with
God. Any change in circumstances would not
bring us into disappointment or distress.

"Jesus answered them, Do ye now believe?
Behold, the hour cometh, yea, is come, that ye shall
be scattered, every man to his own, and shall leave
me alone; and yet I am not alone, because the
Father is with me. These things have I spoken unto
you, that in me ye may have peace. In the world ye
have tribulation: but be of good cheer; I have
overcome the world" (John 16.31–33). At this
juncture these disciples had by this time all believed in the Lord Jesus. Yet the Lord said to them,
"Do ye now believe? . . . Ye shall be scattered,

every man to his own, and shall leave me alone: and yet I am not alone, because the Father is with me." Just as John 17 records the last prayer of the Lord, so John 16 is the last conversation of the Lord with His disciples while on earth. The crystallization of His discourse with them is found in the last few words of chapter 16. The Lord said, "Ye shall be scattered, . . . and shall leave me alone." Were such a situation to happen to us, we would murmur against God, saying, "Why do You leave me alone here?" But the Lord said quietly, "The Father is with me." Naturally speaking, He was entitled to receive some consolation from the disciples who were with Him for so long, yet He did not pin His hope on any of them. And as we well know, though they were all later scattered, He was not in the least hurt by the event. On the contrary, He could tell them—in advance of the event—His own experience so that they might have *peace in Him.* He knew that whoever would drink of the water of this world would thirst again. Therefore, though this water was available for Him, He would not drink of it. Those who refuse to drink of this water will never be thirsty again.

Do We Have a Satisfied Life?

Why do we not have a satisfied life? Why are we disappointed? It is because we have expectations, great expectations. When we fail to get what we have thought would fill us, we are discouraged.

Just here let me give a personal testimony. Many times I have been insulted, and many times I have been praised (even Satan has sometimes praised me). But the Lord reminds me of this verse about our not drinking of this water lest we be thirsty again and become disappointed. When the world affords you affection, help, wealth, fame, comfort, ease, and so forth, you may think that because these are now yours you may drink heartily. But if you do so, you will be thirsty again one day. To the degree that you drink of this world, to that degree will your thirst be.

Some Christians have asked me: "Why do many other people sense the preciousness of the Lord, whereas I do not have such a sense?" I may answer them in this way: "This is due to the fact that aside from the Lord there are many other waters of which you drink. No wonder you do not treasure the Lord." By noting how full is our consecration and how much we have lost of this earth, we will know how much we treasure the Lord.

Paul does not simply say that he has *gained* the Lord as his treasure. He has something to *lose* as well. He counts all things to be loss—he lets go of all things—that he may know and gain the excellency of the Lord Jesus Christ. If you know nothing but Christ, you too will prove how precious and how satisfying is the Lord. In keeping with the spirit of those verses in John 4, we may say that the measure of your loss is the measure of your gain. However much you resist what comes from the world will determine how much you enjoy of the riches of the Lord.

Dear friends, if in your direction people should cast affection, fame, comfort, glory, wealth, and so forth, what will you do? How should you react? Was it true that because she came into possession of the living water the Samaritan woman would no longer drink of the water of this world? No, for she still must drink of the water of this world. We cannot help but drink of this water too. So that when people, friends, and relatives pile glory, fame, wealth, comfort, and help upon us, we may allow them to do so; nevertheless, we should never let ourselves be influenced by these things nor trust ourselves to these folk. Our hearts should not be swayed by these things, neither should we ask anything of the people. If we do not ask for any drink from this source, we will not be disappointed at any time.

I believe that what Isaiah 53.2a speaks concerning the coming Messiah, our Lord Jesus, is most precious: "He grew up before him as a tender plant, and as a root out of a dry ground." What does this mean? In a ground with water, the tree can easily and quickly grow. But the environment the Lord was in did not help Him in this respect at all. There was nothing in *His* environment that would give anything to Him; the world had absolutely nothing with which to help Him. Neither His enemies nor Satan helped Him in the slightest. Even the angels could not help. He received all from God. He did not receive any encouragement, support, or consolation from what was around Him. His life was a straight line.

We know that a straight line is the shortest distance between two points. From this world to the region beyond, our Lord walked a straight path. "No man," He said, "having put his hand to the plow, and looking back, is fit for the kingdom of God" (Luke 9.62). What does this mean? It means that he whose hand is on the plow must have his eyes looking straight ahead, or else the furrow he plows will become crooked. If his eyes look forward, then that which he plows is straight. But if he should glance backwards, what he plows instantly becomes crooked. Oh let us see that God does not wish us to turn aside or to turn about. He alone is to be our satisfaction.

How then can we be satisfied? Listen to what our Lord has declared: "The water which I shall give him shall become in him a well of water springing up unto eternal life" (John 4.14). Outward fame, outward glory, and all such other outward things have no lasting value. Apart from the Lord in us—the Spirit of God in us—nothing can satisfy. How true it is that apart from Him nothing ever satisfies.

I thank and praise Him, because He has traversed life's course for me. He is indeed the beloved Lord!

7 A Deeper Joy

But I said, I have labored in vain, I have spent my strength for nought and vanity; yet surely the justice due to me is with Jehovah, and my recompense with my God. And now saith Jehovah that formed me from the womb to be his servant, to bring Jacob again to him, and that Israel be gathered unto him (for I am honorable in the eyes of Jehovah, and my God is become my strength). (Is. 49.4,5)

At that season Jesus answered and said, I thank thee, O Father, Lord of heaven and earth, that thou didst hide these things from the wise and understanding, and didst reveal them unto babes: yea, Father, for so it was well-pleasing in thy sight. All things have been delivered unto me of my Father: and no one knoweth the Son, save the Father; neither doth any know the Father, save the Son, and he to whomsoever the Son willeth to reveal him. Come unto me, all ye that labor and are heavy laden, and I will give you rest. Take my yoke upon you, and learn of me; for I am meek and lowly in heart: and ye shall find rest unto your souls. For my yoke is easy, and my burden is light. (Matt. 11.25–30)

One

Isaiah is a book of prophecies. Many of its words have reference to Christ. In chapter 49.5 we learn of the kind of work which our Lord does on earth, and in verse 4 we are shown whether or not His work on earth is successful. Why does God send the Lord Jesus to earth? To bring Jacob again to God and again gather Israel to Him. What is the result? It does not appear to be successful. According to man's estimate, our Lord is totally defeated. Jacob has not turned to Him, nor does Israel accept Him. Instead, they reject Him and crucify Him on the cross. Even one of His own disciples betrays Him. Hence it is said here: "I have labored in vain, I have spent my strength for nought and vanity."

Now most likely, were we to find ourselves in such a situation—living on earth as rejected by men, being fruitless in service, and seemingly not accomplishing anything of the will of God—we would at least become negative in our attitude even if we did not become sorrowful or weep with a broken heart. Yet this is not the case with our

Lord, though He does indeed lament, saying, "I have labored in vain, I have spent my strength for nought and vanity." But He equally declares this: "Yet surely the justice due to me is with Jehovah, and my recompense with my God." What does such a word mean? It means that although I have not accomplished what I had expected to, nevertheless I have My justification with Jehovah. I have labored long and seemingly without effect, yet My justice is with God. In other words, whether I am justified in My *work* or not, it is nonetheless there with Jehovah. He is not only My justice but also My recompense. In spite of the fact that I am unable to effect anything with the house of Jacob and the children of Israel, I am certain that I will receive the recompense which God will give to Me. And therefore, I am satisfied in My heart. I shall not murmur nor shall I be sorrowful. Such is the attitude of our Lord.

This, dear friends, shows us one thing: that we should not have any direct relationship with our work, with things, or with people; we can have direct relationship only with God. In the event we maintain a direct connection with work, things, or people, we will be hurt and heartbroken in case we encounter any frustration or difficulty. But if our direct relationship is only with God, we can still rejoice when we are rejected by men, are confronted with difficulty, or suffer apparent defeat. Since we are directly related to God, neither gain nor loss is able to touch us. One thing alone are we careful about: whether or not we have our justice and recompense with God. If our justice is with God, our recompense is also with Him.

Two

That which befalls the Lord and the attitude which He takes towards the events that are recorded in Matthew 11 coincide perfectly with what Isaiah 49 says. All the things told us in Matthew 11 are really quite pathetic. First there is John the Baptist who sends his disciples to inquire of the Lord Jesus, saying, "Art thou he that cometh, or look we for another?" (v.3) In other words, are you truly the Messiah, the Christ that is to come? Here is this forerunner of Jesus who apparently has begun to doubt—"Art thou he that cometh?" This alone, from the human standpoint, would be enough to cause a man to have heartache.

Then, too, John the Baptist is mentioned as coming neither eating nor drinking, and the men of Jesus' day say that John has a demon (see v.18). Moreover, the Son of Man comes eating and drinking; He comes among the same men and mingles with them, hoping to save them. Surely they cannot take issue with this. And yet these same people say: "Behold, a gluttonous man and a winebibber" (v.19)! Here, then, is the sort of people who will say one thing or the other anyway. They will speak against eating as well as against not eating. They have, in fact, an inordinate lust for speaking. Irrespective of what our Lord does, this people will criticize anyway. They condemn His forerunner as having a demon and denounce the Lord as being a gluttonous man and a winebibber. After all the mighty works which He had done in Capernaum, Bethsaida, and Chorazin, these people still reject Him. From the record of Matthew 11 we may conclude that our Lord is One who is doubted, blasphemed, and rejected.

Now what would you do if, in your life and work, you too met with such an unfortunate chain of events perpetrated by the very people with whom you are associated? How could you help but be heartbroken and discouraged, judging that all is lost. Yet not so with our Lord. The Bible reports His attitude at that moment as being this: "At that season Jesus answered and said, I thank thee, O Father, Lord of heaven and earth, that thou didst hide these things from the wise and understanding, and didst reveal them unto babes: yea, Father, for so it was well-pleasing in thy sight." "At that season" means at that particular moment, which is to say, that in the very environment in which He is so doubted, so blasphemed, and so rejected, our Lord is able to pray: "I thank thee, Father, Lord of heaven and earth." There is no bitterness nor sorrow in His heart. He neither frets nor becomes angered. How about you and me, though? Could you and I still thank God even though we are being doubted, slandered, and rejected without cause? Here is a very deep lesson indeed: that we must thank God not only when we obtain something, or when our work prospers, or when we are being admired by many; we must learn to thank Him also when we are doubted, slandered, and rejected without cause. Can you and I thank Him under such an adverse situation?

Our Lord is here thanking God. For what has He to thank Him? Read His words again: "I thank thee, O Father, Lord of heaven and earth, that thou didst hide these things from the wise and understanding, and didst reveal them unto babes." But our Lord adds yet another great comfort to His prayer of thanksgiving, which is: "Yea, Father, for it was well-pleasing in thy sight." Since such is the Father's pleasure, what more can I say? As the Lord Jesus sees this chain of events, they are to be interpreted on this wise: that the doubting of John the Baptist is the Father's good pleasure, that men's criticizing Him as a gluttonous man and a winebibber is the Father's good pleasure, and that even the rejection of Him by several large and important towns is equally the Father's good pleasure. Because He submits himself under the good will of God, He is able to say: "I thank thee, O Father, Lord of heaven and earth." How often you and I cannot even utter the words "O Father", for under such circumstances as these we can hardly believe that God is truly our Father. But our Lord can, because, despite everything, He still senses the intimacy with His Father. But then, too, how often you and I are unable also to say "Lord of heaven and earth" because it seems difficult for you and me to believe that there is one Lord. Yet Jesus is so submissive to God's good will that He can still declare: "O Father, Lord of heaven and earth." Seeing all these circumstances as the Father's good pleasure, He is able to be thankful, and says: "Yea, Father, for so it was well-pleasing in thy sight."

Are you able to say, "Yea, Father, for so it was well-pleasing in thy sight"? When you are being misunderstood or slandered, or you meet with difficulties, do you feel hurt, grow sorrowful, and become heartbroken? Or are you able to submit to the good pleasure of God and raise the voice of thanksgiving? Can you say to Him: "Yea, Father, for so it was well-pleasing in thy sight"? Beloved, can you, will you, say so?

Three

Moreover, the word which our Lord says further in this prayer of thanksgiving seems to explain to us why He could thank God under such environment. Note this that He next declares: "All things have been delivered unto me of my Father: and no one knoweth the Son, save the Father." It is enough as long as the Father knows; that alone is sufficient. It does not really matter at all to Me, the Lord seems to be saying, if the people at Chorazin, at Bethsaida, at Capernaum, or those of the house of Jacob, or of the nation of Israel, or even among those people who have received My help do not know Me. Not even the misunderstanding of John the Baptist really matters. One thing only is important, and that is, "All things have been delivered unto me of my Father: and no one knoweth the Son, save the Father." Oh! If the Father knows, then I am satisfied.

Are you satisfied if God knows you? Or do you still seek to be known by John, by the house of Jacob, and by all Israel? Are you looking for recognition from the people at Capernaum, Bethsaida and Chorazin? If *God* only knows you, is that really enough for you? It is quite true that we need our brothers and our sisters; yet at the time when people do not know us, we will still be satisfied with only the Father's knowledge of us if we are truly those who live before Him.

The Lord Jesus is able to assert: "All things have been delivered unto me of my Father." Let me ask, Is all that you have, given you by the Father? Or do you also receive things from men? Can you honestly say, "O Father, all things have been given me by You"? And can you also say, "O Father, aside from what you give me, I desire nothing from men"? If you are able to declare these words positively, you will undoubtedly be able to rest and to praise.

Not only does the Lord say "No one knoweth the Son save the Father" but also He says "Neither doth any know the Father, save the Son, and he to whomsoever the Son willeth to reveal him." Only the one who is willing to be known by God alone will truly know God; and the one who truly knows God is able to lead other people to know God too. Those who do not know God are incapable of leading other people to Him. Are you thinking of helping others and leading them to the Father? Why is it that your words do not carry weight, why do they fail to move people? For no other reason than because of the fact that what you have is not given you by the Father. You do not deem that which the Father has given you to be sufficient; instead, you belittle what He has delivered to you and seek something further from men. If this is your case, you will not be able to declare that you are only known by the Father. Yet how blessed you will be if in your case it really is sufficient for you to be known only by God himself. Because in that event you will also know God and will be able to lead others to Him.

How can we ever truly know God if we look elsewhere? We do not know Him because we have too many other things. We obtain too much comfort and glory from men to be able to lead people to God. Indeed, if our heart is so full of things other than Him, then we ourselves hardly know Him. Let us remember what the Lord says: "All things have been delivered unto me of my Father: and no one knoweth the Son, save the Father; neither doth any know the Father, save the Son, and he to whomsoever the Son willeth to reveal him." If you and I are able to lay down all these other things in our hearts, we will know God and will also help others to know Him. Our hearts being pure, the pure in heart shall see God (see Matt. 5.8).

Four

After saying the above things, the Lord concludes with those most comforting of words to us; namely, "Come unto me, all ye that labor and are heavy laden, and I will give you rest. Take my yoke upon you, and learn of me; for I am meek and lowly in heart: and ye shall find rest unto your souls. For my yoke is easy, and my burden is light." Our Lord shows us here that His own experience can serve as an example for us, in that, seeing how He has obtained rest, we too may enter into rest.

"Come unto me, all ye that labor and are heavy laden, and I will give you rest." Dear one, is your burden heavy? Are you struggling from dawn to dusk? Do you feel unhappy? Well then, the Lord is saying to you: "Come, come to Me, and I will give you rest." Are there many things that trouble you? Do you realize how unbearable are your burdens? Are you painful over your many failures? "Then come unto me, and I will give you rest," says the Lord.

How does the Lord give us rest? He as it were places himself before us, that we may see Him. He says, "I am meek and lowly." Do we know what meekness is? Meekness means flexibility. He who is meek is able to declare that whatever *God* wants him to have he will have it. Whether to have it or not to have it—all is nonetheless well: having it, he can sing hallelujah and thank God; yet not having it, he still can sing hallelujah and thank God. Meekness is that attitude whereby whatever you have decided upon is subject to change according to God's will. Is the will of God able to change your mind? Are you willing, if God does not agree with you, to lay aside those things which you have decided on, admired, expected, or worked for? You have announced that God loves you, but will you then fret if He does not grant you what you ask for? Can you sing hallelujah anyway? Remember that a meek heart is an obedient heart. So that meekness therefore means that you do not insist on your own view, that you are not stubborn in your thought, neither do you decide on what you want. To have a meek heart signifies that a person is willing to change if indeed God wants him to change. He is ready to turn around if God wants him to return. Whatever change God desires of him, he is open to it. Now such a person as this has perfect rest.

Rest is most precious to life. Some Christians are often restless, dissatisfied, and given to murmuring. One of the causes for such a condition is that they have a desire or a longing which has not been fulfilled. Yet the Lord shows us that the condition for rest is meekness. When the way of

God collides with our own way, are we able to say: "O God, I yield"? If in fact we cannot yield, it reveals our arrogance. How we need to be meek in heart, without which there can be no rest. Do not forget that a meek heart is the first condition for rest.

However, the Lord Jesus is not only meek, He is also lowly. We often conjure up some haughty ideas or carnal wishes. We entertain vain hopes and unprofitable plans. We love to compare ourselves with other brothers or sisters, becoming unhappy if they should walk ahead of us. We strive to be higher and greater than others. We are conceited in our thought and insolent in our heart. We are totally unlike our Lord Jesus—whose heart is meek and lowly, whose eyes are never haughty, and whose expectations are never for himself but who is willing to accept whatever God has given Him. He can say that this is enough, that all is well. Such demeanor shows how lowly is His heart. Are you, though, content with that which God has given you? Or are you thinking all the time to gain more? God is looking for those who are lowly in heart. Many are so ambitious and high-minded that God is not able to use them. Their heart being arrogant, they can find no rest.

We need to consider whether our decision is subject to any change. Are we able to change our opinion, our expectation and our thought—for God's sake? If we are ambitious of getting this or that thing, then our heart is neither meek nor lowly. A humble person will accept whatever God gives. He is able to say hallelujah and to offer thanks to the Lord concerning anything the Lord may be pleased to give. Being meek, our Lord Jesus is soft and tender before God. Being lowly, He makes no demand for himself. Only a meek person is able to receive guidance from God; only a lowly person can satisfy God's heart.

"Take my yoke upon you," says the Lord, "and learn of me; for I am meek and lowly in heart: and ye shall find rest unto your souls." He tells us His own experience so that we may see that by taking up His yoke and learning of Him we too may find rest. Our biggest problem lies in our dislike of God's will. This is why we have neither rest nor joy within. The Bible shows us two kinds of joy: one is that which comes from believing in God's grace, and the other is that which results from obeying God's will. We all believe in God's grace, but are we willing to obey God's will? Let me ask this of you: Are you unhappy in your heart? Are you dissatisfied? Are you complaining because something fails to suit your plan, expectation, or thought? If so, there can be only one reason, which is, that you are unwilling to obey God's will.

The person who has had some spiritual experience will agree that nothing is more joyous than consecration, nothing can surpass the joy of putting himself in God's hand and allowing Him to manage his life. In case you are unhappy and dissatisfied in your heart, it must be due to the fact that you have not taken the Lord's yoke nor have you learned from Him. The joy of committing all to the Lord is a deeper joy. It is the joy of knowing that all things have been delivered to you by the Father and the joy of being able to say: "Yea, Father, for so it was well-pleasing in thy sight." This is what our Lord's experience has conveyed to us.

Five

If you have no rest or joy, you must be holding on to something which you are unwilling to give up. People feel despondent because there is something troubling them. Is there anything in you that is disturbing you? Anything which you dare not question, nor even think about? Many Christians do not have the courage to look within for fear of seeing something. When God touches them, they try to evade the issue and dare not sit quietly for a few minutes to think it over. They struggle and become perplexed, experiencing neither rest nor joy.

Nonetheless, if you are really willing to take up the Lord's yoke and learn of Him, you will be filled with joy and praise. Once a brother in leaving his town to preach the gospel in a distant land declared: "Hereafter I shall be separated far away from my relatives, family and friends"; but then he continued on with another word: "I am the happiest person in the world!" Some of us probably know only the joy of salvation; this brother, though, knew also the joy of consecration. In the latter case it is quite true that often our hearts will ache, yet our mouths are full of words of praise. Is it not a pity that the sound of praise in numerous Christians is blocked by so many things? This does not necessarily mean there are sins; it may simply indicate that there are too many things besides God. If they would only allow the Lord to get rid of these obstructions, their hearts would find rest and they would be filled with joy.

Many brothers and sisters maintain too deep a relationship with people. Such a relationship with man surpasses even their relationship with God. Consequently, when one day they lose the love of man or the favor of man, they likewise lose their rest and joy. What would they say and how would they feel if they were confronted with a chain of events full of misunderstanding, slander, and rejection perpetrated by men? Would not some of them begin to reason with God and get into controversy with Him? And as a result they would find no rest or joy in their hearts. But if they were able to come before God and to pray: "O God, I will say amen and yes to all the things which You have permitted to befall me", they would be filled instantly with heavenly rest and joy.

Once a brother was traveling through the wilderness in the moonlight. God spoke to him, saying: "How about My taking away from you what you have?" "O God, I cannot," he answered.

But God then said to him, "You are weak,
therefore you cannot; but what if I enable you to
do so?" Immediately the brother replied: "God, I
thank You and praise You that though I cannot,
yet You can." He was willing to let God do the
work, he was willing to submit to the will of God.
He shed tears on the one hand but committed all to
God on the other. Strangely, as soon as he yielded
he was filled with the joy and peace of heaven.

Have you ever tasted such joy and peace as
this? The Lord is waiting to grant you such joy and
peace. But the key question is: Are you willing to
take the Lord's yoke and learn of Him? Because of
your dissatisfaction with the Lord's demand on
you, you are today without the blessing of the Lord
and you cannot channel the Lord's blessing to
other people. "My yoke is easy, and my burden is
light," says the Lord. Do you believe this word?
Whoever does not know God will complain that
God is too hard, reaping where He does not sow
and gathering where He does not scatter; but
whoever knows God will confess that the Lord's
yoke is indeed easy and the Lord's burden is
indeed light.

How bewildering that many of God's children
are afraid to learn about His will. They sing
hallelujah when they hear of the love of God, His
wisdom and power; but they are somewhat fearful
when it comes to hearing about the will of God.
Let us notice what our Lord's attitude is. As
regards the will of God, He does not say "God's

will" but says "well-pleasing in Thy sight." For Him, all of God's wills are good. Oh dear friends, let us be those who truly believe in God's loving heart. Let us believe that without a doubt He loves us, and that therefore whatever may come to us we are able to be at rest about it.

Frequently we ask for fish and God seemingly gives us a serpent; we ask for bread and He appears to be giving us a stone. So we inquire why this is so. The fact is that we oftentimes think we do ask for fish, not knowing that what we are actually asking for is a serpent. What God gives us may look like a serpent indeed, but it is really fish nonetheless. Many times we seem to ask for bread, yet without realizing that in actual fact we are asking for a stone; and so what God gives us may appear to be a stone whereas in truth it is bread. Frequently we fancy that He has not answered our prayer and does not love us; in point of fact, though, God is going to give us the best. Oh let us acknowledge that our God can make no mistake. If there is any mistake at all it is that many people just do not believe the love of God. Let us be clear that, yes, sometimes God does permit sorrowful and difficult situations to come upon us; yet this is not because He does not love us, but because He wants to give us the best so that He may build us up. Oh! Were we to believe that all things come to us through the good will of God, we would sing with tears.

We believe not only in God's love, we believe

also in His wisdom. He loves us and He knows all. His love never changes, His wisdom never fails. And thus nothing that is unprofitable will ever happen to us. We must also believe that His power is well able to carry us through whatever He purposes for us as well as to strengthen us to endure everything. Thus may we say before Him: "Thank You and praise You, O God, for Your will is perfect." Praising God for His grace marks the beginning of praise; but praising Him for His will perfects the lesson of praise. To praise God for what is gained is to initiate a person into praise, but to praise Him for what is lost is to complete that person in praise. Let us see that we are able to rest and to be joyful because all things are saturated with the wisdom and power of God as well as with His love.

There is the following word in the daily devotional book called *Streams in the Desert* for the day of October 24th: "A bar of steel worth five dollars, when wrought into horseshoes, is worth ten dollars. If made into needles, it is worth three hundred and fifty dollars; if into penknife blades, it is worth thirty-two thousand dollars; if into springs for watches it is worth two hundred and fifty thousand dollars." Do you understand the explanation for this difference between 10 dollars, 350 dollars, 32,000 dollars and 250,000 dollars? The same raw material is being refined and beaten so that it becomes increasingly more resilient, having more strength and more worth. In order that we may be more valuable, God causes us to undergo more refinings and beatings.

If we wish to be a useful and valuable vessel before God, we should not murmur but instead be joyful and restful towards all the things that He permits to come upon us. Let us say to God: "O Father, I thank You; for all that You have permitted to come upon me is good." By submitting ourselves to the will of God our hearts shall find rest. We will be filled with joy, and our mouths shall also be full of praise. Our burden will no longer be heavy.

We have now seen that our Lord Jesus had within Him a deeper joy. It was because He trusted in God: "Yet surely the justice due to me is with Jehovah, and my recompense with my God." Also, because of His attitude towards God's will: "Yea, Father, for so it was well-pleasing in thy sight." And so the Lord clearly tells us to do this: "Take my yoke upon you, and learn of me; for I am meek and lowly in heart: and ye shall find rest unto your souls." If we desire to share in this deeper joy we must believe in the Lord's word, be willing to take up His yoke and to learn of Him. And we can then give thanks to the Lord, because His yoke *is* easy and His burden *is* light. Praise His name!

8 Rest Is Power

Now as they went on their way, he entered into a certain village: and a certain woman named Martha received him into her house. And she had a sister called Mary, who also sat at the Lord's feet, and heard his word. But Martha was cumbered about much serving; and she came up to him, and said, Lord, dost thou not care that my sister did leave me to serve alone? bid her therefore that she help me. But the Lord answered and said unto her, Martha, Martha, thou art anxious and troubled about many things: but one thing is needful: for Mary hath chosen the good part, which shall not be taken away from her. (Luke 10.38–42)

For thus said the Lord Jehovah, the Holy One of Israel, In returning and rest shall ye be saved; in quietness and in confidence shall be your strength. (Is. 30.15)

In nothing be anxious; but in everything by prayer and supplication with thanksgiving let your requests be made known unto God. And the peace of God, which passeth all understanding, shall guard your hearts and your thoughts in Christ Jesus. (Phil. 4.6,7)

Take my yoke upon you, and learn of me; for I am meek and lowly in heart: and ye shall find rest unto your souls. (Matt. 11.29)

One

One day on His earthly travels our Lord Jesus entered a village where a sister called Martha received Him to her house. This sister loved our Lord, so she wanted to do things for Him in order to please Him. Thus she went on to do this and that, preparing things for the Lord. Being pressed by this business, she became disturbed, grew worried and even annoyed. She was like anybody else, in that when something was wrong within her she began to blame others. She therefore came to the Lord and complained: "Lord, dost thou not care that my sister did leave me to serve alone? bid her therefore that she help me." The Lord replied: "Martha, Martha, thou art anxious and troubled about many things: but one thing is needful: for Mary hath chosen the good part, which shall not be taken away from her." Oh, the Lord declared that only one thing was needful! Martha did many things, but the Lord said that only one thing was needful, not many. You are planning to do this thing and that thing. You are doing this and that as though there were many plans to be laid and many things to be done; but one thing alone is needful. Not so many things, only one thing!

What is the one thing needful? None other than Christ himself, whom Mary herself had chosen. How can we obtain this one needful thing? By sitting quietly at the Lord's feet; and this was exactly what Mary did. Each one of us Christians must do something. The Bible even tells us that "if any will not work, neither let him eat" (2 Thess. 3.10). We *should* work, and diligently so. Yet frequently while we are working we have no rest in us, as though we have forgotten the Lord. We are so busy from morning till night that we have not really prayed and studied God's word. The motive for our labors, many spiritual works, and helps rendered to this brother or that sister is undoubtedly for the Lord's sake; yet somehow these activities cause inward problems, and mental disturbances develop afterwards. The difficulty lies in the fact that many affairs tend to make us forgetful of the Lord. Let us therefore listen to what the Lord says—"But one thing is needful"! And this thing is to rest in the Lord, which, if done, ends up in our being satisfied with the Lord.

Two

How, then, can we live a peaceful and tranquil life? To answer this, we must see what the Lord says. He has not said that we should not work, nor has He said that we should work but half a day and spend the other half in spiritual things. He has not reprimanded Martha, saying that it is wrong for her to do many things. What the Lord reminds her of is, that she should not allow herself to be anxious or troubled over many things. The Lord Jesus does not say she has done too much; He only mentions that she has thought too much, worried too much. You may work from morning till night, but you should not be anxious and troubled all the day. Many people are not really too busy with outward things, though they are fairly busy inwardly. Some will be so anxious and busily occupied in their mind concerning the thing which is to happen five days later that they lose five nights rest in the process. Suppose it will take you but one hour to visit someone tomorrow, yet you dream about this for four hours at night. Then you are thinking too much. The Lord does not charge us not to do things: He only enjoins us not to be anxious and troubled while we *do* them. He does not say we have done too much; He merely says that we ought not be anxious and troubled.

This is the Christian life: that we ought to work diligently and not be lazy. It is right for us to labor hard, and it is not detrimental to be busy outwardly. Yet what is of vital importance is for us to be calm inwardly. Only one thing is allowed within—none other than Christ himself. And this is what the Lord Jesus is showing us here. The Lord requires but one thing of us, which is, that in the midst of whatever circumstance, we are not to be touched by it. Physically we may toil hard and do many things, but inwardly there is no loosening up in the matter of our having this one thing. Outwardly we can be fully engrossed, yet inwardly we maintain constant fellowship with God. Thank God, there is not only a Martha but there is also a Mary. Mary has chosen the good part, which is communion with the Lord. The Lord wants Martha to learn from her sister this matter of inner rest, not learn from her sister to do things. We can be Martha outwardly but never inwardly. Outwardly we may be Martha but inwardly we must learn to be Mary in having perfect union with the Lord. Though busily engaged outwardly, there is calm fellowship with God inwardly. This is a most precious experience.

Take brother Lawrence for example. He had to prepare meals from morning till evening for many people. Now if this were our situation, we probably would be so busy as to lose our fellowship with God. Yet brother Lawrence maintained such an inner communion with the Lord that outside things did not affect him at all. How truly he was one who knew the presence of the Lord. Outwardly he was busy all the time, yet inwardly he continually sat at God's feet. He had many things to do externally, but he was not perturbed in the least by these outside concerns.

This is the kind of precious life we all need.

Every one of us can have such a life. This life finds its source in the depths of our being, not in our feeling or action. There in our depths is a constant fellowship with the Lord, a tranquil and steady life in the Lord. We must always remember that God has not called us to be lazy and do nothing. He intends to dwell in us so that we are able to stand the hustle and bustle of life. We may be busily occupied from sunrise to sunset; yet however much we toil nothing can cause us to lose the inward peace, nothing can deprive us of the river of rest. Externally we are busy, but internally there is rest.

Hence never allow outside matters to touch you. You must resist the intrusion of outward things upon you. Whatever these external affairs may be, you must not let them penetrate to your depths. In you there is only one person, even Christ; within you there is only one exercise, to be near to Christ. If you permit any other thing to intrude, you will soon lose your inward peace.

Three

The tabernacle in the Old Testament period is divided into the outer court, the holy place, and the Holy of Holies. In the Holy of Holies is the ark which is the dwelling place of God. In the holy place are the table of showbread, the golden candlestick, and the golden altar of incense; while in the court are the altar and the laver. A veil separates the Holy of Holies from the holy place; a screen, between the holy place and the court; and still another screen, between the court and the outside world. The Levites and the priests may enter the court; only the priests may enter the holy place; and the high priest alone may enter the Holy of Holies once a year with the blood.

In the New Testament time, we are told by God through His servants that we are the temple of God (see 1 Cor. 3.16). The life of the Christian resembles the situation in God's tabernacle of old. The court outside is extremely busy. With thousands upon thousands of the children of Israel, the offerings they present must be innumerable. Think of the immense number of Levites who will be slaughtering bullocks and sheep, and the enormous amount of time they will spend in doing so. The court may, in fact, be filled to overflowing with people from morning till evening; whereas in the Holy of Holies there is not a man to be found. The screen of the court may be raised time after time to let many people in, but the veil for the Holy of Holies remains hanging low, without the slightest movement nor the letting in of anyone. The court may be resounding with noises; the Holy of Holies, however, is absolute quiet. In the court are the din and bustle of activity, but the Holy of Holies is totally unaffected. Such is the Christian life. On the outside you may be in touch with thousands of people, but you yourself can still be the calmest and the most unperturbed of persons; busy outwardly, yet not a ripple of disturbance in the spirit;

externally engrossed in works, yet internally deep in fellowship with the Lord. This is how to have rest in the spirit.

We Christians should be living in incessant prayer. It is not merely praying for ten minutes or half an hour; nor just praying in the morning after rising up and then forgetting to pray while working. Since we live before the Lord, we are in communion with Him inwardly and continually, however busily occupied we may be outwardly. We should indeed have a fixed time for prayer and for Bible reading; but besides these fixed times, our inner life should continually be in fellowship with the Lord.

Let us remember that the strength for our walk depends entirely upon the communion maintained between our innermost life and God. The innermost place is not at all governed or influenced by the outside. Being *inwardly* calm, we are then able to control all the things outwardly. Although there are no candlestick, no altar of incense, and no showbread in the Holy of Holies, this innermost place nonetheless controls all the movements of the tabernacle. So that if there is a tranquil life present in the Holy of Holies, none of these outer things and circumstances can shake us. By living in the Holy of Holies we shall see that God has permeated all things. Our relationship with God is constantly attuned; nothing from the outside can interrupt it.

Four

Too often we have a failure in our lives, which is, that our inside becomes disturbed as we are busy outside. Frequently, before there is much toiling outwardly, we are already troubled inwardly. Due to inner agitation, we have no power to cope with outer things. We ought to know that the strength of our life lies in rest and in quietness. The word of God says: "In returning and rest shall ye be saved; in quietness and in confidence shall be your strength." No one who is easily excited has much strength before God, neither does that one who is anxious and troubled in mind have much power. Let us always remember that our strength lies in quietness and in confidence.

In each hurricane which occurs there is an eye. Although the wind swirls swiftly at the circumference, the eye deep within is most calm. Such a life of quietness in the center is our strength. Though outward things blow fiercely as do hurricanes, yet within us there is perfect calm. "In quietness and in confidence shall be your strength." Never allow your mind to be troubled by the abundance of external things, because you will surely lose your tranquillity, and thus lose control over your environment.

Observe the sea, and note that however much may be the changes at its surface—the waves may rage high and the wind may blow strong—in its depths there is not the slightest motion but all is perfect calm. Some people specialize in the study of organisms located at the bottom of the sea; and the study of these organisms has shown that the sea bottom has not undergone change for a great number of years. In like manner, the life of the Christian is characterized by a similar deep inner quietness and lack of disturbance. We cannot hope for a leisurely life, yet we can expect to be able to keep very calm in the midst of much activity. We may even undertake a little more work, yet within us there is that quietness and confidence. The peace that we have available to us is an inner peace. And were there actually such peace operating within us, we would not be defeated. Whatever circumstance we may find ourselves in, we will still live before the Lord as though nothing else matters. We see the Lord who is in us, and He it is who enables us to live a restful life.

Please note that our Lord was never affected by any outside influence. On one occasion the people in the synagogue persecuted Him, and even tried thereafter to push Him down a cliff. Now if this had ever happened to us, we would immediately have run away. But the Bible states that He, "passing through the midst of them went his way" (Luke 4.30). These people wished to take His life, but He walked through their midst as though He could not have cared less.

Another time, there arose a great tempest in the sea, insomuch that the boat was covered with the waves; but our Lord was asleep! The disciples cried out, "Save, Lord; we perish"! Why did they cry out? Because they had no rest in them. But our Lord was not stirred up at all by the situation (see Matt. 8.23–27).

And later on, when a band of soldiers and officers came to seize Him with torches and weapons, the Lord stepped forth and asked them, "Whom seek ye?" "Jesus of Nazareth," they answered. Jesus said to them, "I am he." When they heard this word, they went backward and fell to the ground. These who were to seize the Lord were terrified by the seized one (see John 18.2–6). Oh, He who is the Lord blessed forever is never moved by external things, since He always lives by His inner life.

Five

How, then, can *we* obtain this inner rest? The following Scripture verses tell us of two conditions:

Here is the first condition—that "in nothing be anxious; but in everything by prayer and supplication with thanksgiving let your requests be made known unto God. And the peace of God, which passeth all understanding, shall guard your hearts and your thoughts in Christ Jesus" (Phil. 4.6,7). The first condition for obtaining rest is to make your requests known to God. You may tell Him of your work, your need, and the difficulty you have. "Lord, I commit all these to Your hand." Whenever you are confronted with these things, you commit them to God by prayer and supplication with thanksgiving, and the peace of God shall garrison your heart and thought. The task of garrisoning is undertaken by God. Your task is simply to make your requests known to Him by prayer and supplication with thanksgiving. As things come your way, you immediately commit them to God. As you commit them, His peace garrisons you at once. At the very moment that you commit the matter to God, the peace of God comes to you. Thus from morning till night you will not be affected by outside things. However great is the difficulty and however many are the problems, the peace of God shall garrison your heart all the time.

And the second condition is—"Take my yoke upon you, and learn of me; for I am meek and lowly in heart: and ye shall find rest unto your souls" (Matt. 11.29). The first condition is faith, the second condition is obedience. God permits many things to befall you, and if you resist what He intends for you, despising His will and desiring something else, you will not find rest within you. We should know that rest comes from consecration. If, when difficulty comes your way, you will but take the Lord's yoke and learn of Him, you will have rest—even though you feel pained because you cannot do what you will. By telling the Lord, "Lord, I am willing to take whatever You give," you will surely find rest. But if you are not willing and instead decide to choose your own way, live your own life, and keep your own hope, you will certainly lose your rest. All your dissatisfactions and desires cause you to lose your rest. Yet were you to say to the Lord, "Lord, whatever You give me is good; I am willing to go Your way, do Your will, and lay aside my own expectation," your heart shall indeed be filled with rest.

May the Lord give us grace, causing us to believe that He is able to bear all our burdens and problems and causing us to yield to all His will for us. May we say "I am willing" to whatever demand God may put upon us. May the Lord help us to see clearly that rest comes only by trust and obedience. While the heart of unbelief remains, rest will never come. When desiring anything for our own sake, rest will not come. But if we believe and trust God, nothing whatever on the outside can disturb our heart. By maintaining constant fellowship with the Lord we will be able to bear all things. May we truly see that rest is power.

9 Christ's Mind Our Mind

If there is therefore any exhortation in Christ, if any consolation of love, if any fellowship of the Spirit, if any tender mercies and compassions, make full my joy, that ye be of the same mind, having the same love, being of one accord, of one mind; doing nothing through faction or through vainglory, but in lowliness of mind each counting other better than himself; not looking each of you to his own things, but each of you also to the things of others. Have this mind in you, which was also in Christ Jesus: who, existing in the form of God, counted not the being on an equality with God a thing to be grasped, but emptied himself, taking the form of a servant, being made in the likeness of men; and being found in fashion as a man, he humbled himself, becoming obedient even unto death, yea, the death of the cross. (Phil. 2.1–8)

This is a passage which we who are Christians must reckon with.

Verse 1: "If there is therefore any exhortation in Christ, if any consolation of love, if any fellowship of the Spirit, if any tender mercies and compassions." This verse is deep in meaning. It may be taken as the foundation, nourishment, and spring of the verses which follow. Without this verse, the following verses can hardly be practiced. Hence a proper understanding of this first verse will facilitate such practice.

"If there is therefore . . . in Christ." These are very significant words. What Paul means is that if there is any exhortation in Christ there will quite naturally be the same mind as well. If there is any consolation of love, there will spontaneously be the same love. If there be any fellowship of the Spirit and any tender mercies and compassions, then there will unquestionably be one accord and one mind. Contrariwise, though, if there is no exhortation in Christ, there can never be the same mind; if there is no consolation of love, there cannot be the same love; and if no fellowship and no compassions, then no one accord and one mind. In short, with these things in Christ, there can be the other things in us; without them in Christ, there will not be anything in us.

Paul writes this first verse to convey the source, the foundation, and the nutrient for what is to follow. Suppose he exhorts the brothers and sisters in Philippi to be of the same mind, have the same love, be of one accord and one mind, and do nothing through faction or vainglory but in lowliness of mind count others better and care for the things of others, and yet he does not give them this verse one. How, then, will they answer him? Most probably they will say: Although all these are good, we simply are unable to do them. Christ is able, but how can we do them without the power of Christ? I have my own mind, and others have their minds; I have my own thought, but so do the others. How can we possibly be one? For this reason Paul first tries to solve their difficulty by telling them, "If there is therefore . . . in Christ." If so, then all these things can be easily done. To make one full, he needs to be fed first; to make one strong, he must be given the strength first. Hence in this initial verse Paul shows us that there is a power in Christ. Because I am in Christ, therefore I am able. Outside of Christ, I am only a sinner; but *in* Christ I am saved. Outside of Christ, I am defeated; but *in* Christ I am victorious. How truly very meaningful are the words "in Christ"!

Verse 2: "Make full my joy, that ye be of the same mind, having the same love, being of one accord, of one mind." Is it at all possible for two persons to be of the same mind? If two brothers are together, can they be of one mind? Is it that A is to change his mind to fit in with B's, or vice versa? What if there are 5 persons, or 500, or even 1000?

The difficulty seems to intensify as the number of people involved increases. How can all these minds be of one accord? For whenever they wish to do anything, one has his opinion and another has his way. Are you to submit to me, or I to you? A may think that B should submit to him; but B may reflect upon the matter and feel that A should be the one to submit. Neither of these is God's way. For the way of God is stated in verse 5: "Have this mind in you, which was also in Christ Jesus." It is not that A is to lay aside his mind to suit B, nor that B is to set aside his mind to meet A. Rather, it is a having the mind of Christ in the midst in order that both A and B may be of one mind with Him. If every mind is in line with Christ's, then it is very easy for all to be of one accord despite the great number of people involved.

Were we to be of one accord and one mind we would not only gladden God's heart but also make His joy full. Paul is here speaking on God's behalf. Only when believers manifest such a condition will the heart of God and of Christ be full of joy. Many things may *gladden* the Lord, but only the one accord among the Christians can make His joy *full.* Winning souls for Christ may give Him joy: living victoriously may also give Him joy: but only the one mind among His people will make His joy full.

This verse is concerned mainly with the mind. To be of one mind is an inward matter; it is not primarily something outward. Not only the mouths speak the same thing, but also the minds think the same thing. Some people can only say with their mouths that they are one; their minds, though, are far from it. They can be at variance in their minds and so different in their attitudes that the spectators can easily detect their disunity; nevertheless, they will still declare with their mouths that they are of one accord. Such kind of one mind is not what God wants at all. God will so work in us that our oneness is not only in the mouth but also in the mind. This oneness of mind is based on the "in Christ" of verse 1. For only in Christ is such one accord possible.

Verse 3: "Doing nothing through faction or through vainglory, but in lowliness of mind each counting other better than himself." What is a faction? It is a small group of people inclined to act for party purposes, which is to say that a faction is a small group that is in reality outside of the Lord. What kind of glory is vainglory? Please note that the Bible speaks of "an eternal weight of glory" (2 Cor. 4.17), a glory which is weighty or substantial, permanent and unfading. Such an eternal weight of glory only God alone has. Therefore, whatever glory is not weighty and permanent is vainglory. Even though not all men possess this vainglory, all undoubtedly are looking for it.

Unfortunately, sometimes there arises dissension among brothers and sisters. Now if such dissension is not due to faction, it must be due to vainglory. Each aspires to be great, and none will prefer the other in honor. Actually, thinking to be great may not make one great, for there will yet be someone even greater.

Negatively speaking, we should not do anything through faction or vainglory; positively, though, we should "in lowliness of mind each count the other better than himself." What is lowliness? Lowliness is a not leaving any room for oneself. Whoever leaves some room for himself can never be said to be lowly. He who insists on his authority or right is not a humble man. Lowliness is also a matter of the mind. *Speaking* lowly words may not necessarily confirm a lowliness in *mind.* Many things may pass through the mouth without their having previously passed through the mind. Lowliness in mind must of necessity come from within.

How is this lowliness of mind expressed in attitude? It is only made evident in a man "counting other better than himself." This is the sign of lowliness. How very difficult it is to count other better than oneself! Once a brother asked an elderly Christian who had served the Lord for many decades: "What is the most difficult of all the Christian virtues?" His answer was Philippians 2.3: "In lowliness of mind each counting other better than himself"—this was the most difficult of all. It is indeed hard to be humble! Let us not forget what sin it was that caused Lucifer to become the devil. Was it not pride? Lucifer fell because he wanted to be equal with God (see Is. 14.14). Moreover, what sin was it which the devil used to entice man to fall? That too was pride. For the devil told man that he could be as God, knowing good and evil (see Gen. 3.5). So that man ate and he too fell. In view of all this, it must be said that lowliness is certainly the most difficult of all virtues.

How can a person count the other as more excellent than himself? One Christian has well said: "In looking at myself, I look at my old man; in looking at another, I look at his new man." Truly, if we look at our own natural life with its corruption, while looking at the grace of God in others and seeing the changes which it has wrought in them, we cannot help but count others better than ourselves. From the human standpoint it is quite true that the Christians in Rome would be greatly helped by Paul were he to visit them; even so, Paul, still remaining separated from them, could see how their faith was being proclaimed throughout the whole world, so that he too was helped by the work of God in them (see Rom. 1.8).

How frequently we think so little of others. Our expectations of them are even higher than the Lord's! This is because what we see are their obvious failures; but what the Lord sees are their hidden victories. We observe that so-and-so has clearly failed once, twice, even ten times over; by contrast, the Lord notices that he has overcome secretly once, twice, even a hundred times. You may be tempted five times and fail five times; he may be tempted thrice and fail but once. Possibly he has had many victories in secret which you have never seen—nor which you have ever had yourself. You may have had *ten* encounters and failed only once, but he may have had a *hundred* battles and only failed once. If we understand this, can we not count others better than ourselves?

Verse 4: "Not looking each of you to his own things, but each of you also to the things of others." This is not at all easy to practice. Oftentimes we seem to be hardly able to take care of our own things, so how can we look after the things of other people? To look after the things of others is a sacrificial life. There was once a brother who exhibited a rare quality: Whenever someone came to see him, he looked as though he had nothing else to do but to treat his visitor's concern as the most important thing of that moment. Actually, though, on that very day he had to write quite a few letters, interview numerous people, and undertake many tasks. Nevertheless, he would look after other people's things as though he had nothing else to occupy his time and interest. This is really denying oneself. How greatly the Lord looked after the things of others! He even went to the extent of dying because we had sinned. Had He been as cold, indifferent, and careless as we often are, where would we be today? We need to learn how to look after the things of others.

Verse 5: "Have this mind in you, which was

also in Christ Jesus." This short statement summarizes verses one through four. If we take the mind of Christ as our mind, all things are then possible. What is the mind of Jesus Christ? Paul answers us with the words that follow.

Verses 6 and 7: "Who, existing in the form of God, counted not the being on an equality with God a thing to be grasped, but emptied himself, taking the form of a servant, being made in the likeness of men." This first part—"Who, existing in the form of God, counted not the being on an equality with God a thing to be grasped"—constitutes the legal rights of Christ which He verily deserved to have. Yet the second part—"but emptied himself, taking the form of a servant, being made in the likeness of men"—conveys to us what is the mind of Christ. What then is this mind? It is that mind in Christ that is willing to set aside His legal rights. Perhaps you are reflecting on how people ought to treat you. But what Christ unquestionably deserves to have, He willingly has not. He is equal with God by nature, yet He emptied himself so as to take the form of a slave and be made in the likeness of men. And such is the mind of Christ.

The "form of a servant" speaks of the lowliness of the Lord; the "likeness of men" speaks of the human limitation the Lord suffers himself to have. The form of a slave is in contrast with the form of God; while man is set forth here in contrast to

God. The form of God is glorious, whereas the form of a servant is lowly. God is unlimited, but man is limited by space, time, food, and rest. Thus the mind of Christ is herein manifested in His willingness to humble himself and to accept limitation. The Lord announced, "I and the Father are one" (John 10.30); but He also declared, "The Father is greater than I" (John 14.28). Is there any inequality in the triune God? Most definitely not. The so-called great or small is not something inherent in the Godhead, but rather is something that comes through voluntary desire.

Verse 8: "And being found in fashion as a man, he humbled himself, becoming obedient even unto death, yea, the death of the cross." The obedience of the Lord is to One who is His equal. His obedience is a being obedient out of His heart unto death, even the death of the cross.

Once a sister met a very lively brother who was learned, well acquainted with the Scriptures, and quite moving in his preaching. Nevertheless, this sister said to him, "Brother, the word you preach is right, but the way you walk is wrong." Whereupon this brother replied, "I preach the word of the cross and stress that we should deny ourselves and take up the cross." "You indeed so preach, but I observe that you have never died," said the sister. Fortunately, he was humble enough to be instructed, so that the sister could help him according to the word of God. Later on he wrote a letter to the sister, saying: "After you left, I said to God, 'I do not know what the cross and the way of the cross are, and what a denying of self is. O God, in my ignorance I offer myself to You that You may enable me to deny self.' So my problems came. My wife began to oppose me. And when I found the situation unbearable, a voice within spoke to me, saying, 'You are to deny self in these things, you are to die.' Formerly, I spoke on the cross and on self-denial, though I knew not where and how to die. But now I know, for I today see that the cross has to be lived out in one's daily life. Hereafter, as I commence to speak in this way, I arouse the opposition of many people. But I am convinced that I need to die in the midst of my colleagues." Oh how many believers do realize that they should deny self, but the question is, where to die. This brother discovered that it must be in the midst of one's colleagues; that to die to self is to die among those whom you can see and touch.

May God bless us that we may take the mind of Christ Jesus as our mind, that we may live a life of peace and love, and so make the joy of the Lord full and complete.

10 The Sympathy of the High Priest

For we have not a high priest that cannot be touched with the feeling of our infirmities; but one that hath been in all points tempted like as we are, yet without sin. Let us therefore draw near with boldness unto the throne of grace, that we may receive mercy, and may find grace to help us in time of need. (Heb. 4.15,16)

The Lord Jesus was tempted in all things while He was here on earth. He felt the pain in sufferings; He experienced heartache when misunderstood. Great were the afflictions He endured and many were the persecutions He met. Having had the same feelings as we do during various temptations, He is now ever sympathetic to our infirmities.

The Lord is sympathetic towards the infirmities of men, but He is never soft on sins. Do remember that He is "without sin". He has been tempted in all points like as we are, except that He is without sin. Never does He say: "I am sympathetic to the sin you commit, therefore I forgive you." What He is touched with is man's infirmities. What are the infirmities of the human race? Well, besides the sufferings of our flesh there are the weaknesses in the areas of our soul. The Lord is kind and understanding towards such infirmities. He is sympathetic to the sufferings of our body and the distresses in our soul.

To be sympathetic means to feel what others feel. Have you ever felt the feeling of other people? Are you at all sympathetic to others? Many times you may be helping people, yet you have no heart of sympathy towards them; that is to say, you are not touched with their sufferings. You may extend material helps to those in need, but you have never felt the distress of their lives. You may feed and clothe and serve the sick, but you do not sense their pains. Though there seems to be grace outwardly, there may not be sympathy inwardly, for you do not feel as they feel.

Jesus is not only the Lord of grace, He is also a most sympathetic Lord. The Bible gives two titles to Him: one is the Savior of sinners; the other, the friend of sinners (see Matt. 11.19). As Savior He redeems sinners; as friend, He communicates with sinners and feels the pains and sorrows of sinners.

Thank and praise God, the Lord Jesus is not only the Savior of sinners but the friend of sinners as well. Herein are we shown a little more of His rich glory. Sometimes you encounter trouble, you feel lonely, you are distressed with the faces people show you, your heart is broken by the many voices and whispers—everything looks so bleak to you; nevertheless, you should know that when the billows roar and the waves run high over you, the Lord is not only your Savior, He is also your friend! He feels *every*thing that you feel. He is sympathetic to you, and He goes through all these matters with you.

Sympathy is characteristic of the life of our Lord on earth. The Bible records many times His sympathy with men. Touched with sympathy, He healed the sick. He fed the hungry by giving bread to five thousand and then to four thousand. He opened the eyes of the blind when He heard the cry, "Have mercy on us, thou son of David" (Matt. 9.27). He bade the dead to rise when He witnessed the mourning of the relatives. Oh that our hearts may be open to see how the Lord's sympathy is poured out upon us! Before He becomes the Savior of sinners, He is already the friend of sinners. Now we of course know that our Lord came to this world to die. Yet had death been *our* mission in being born into this world, we would have met this appointed death but cared for nothing else. Not so, though, with our Lord. Although the cross was already clearly set before Him, nevertheless, before that time finally arrived, He showed sympathy to all those who needed Him even as He was journeying towards His death. Oh what a merciful Lord!

To be sympathetic with other people three factors are indispensable. First is experience. Before you can appreciate a situation, you must first have experienced it. For example, if you have never been sick, can you really be understanding towards the sick? If you have never had a toothache, you will not be able to sympathize with those having a toothache. If you have never had a headache, will you be able to feel the misery of a headache? Not having experienced pain, you are unable to feel as the sufferer feels; and therefore you cannot sympathize with him. Experience is essential, because it helps you to be able to show sympathy to others.

A sister once complained: "Many things I find hard to overcome, and so I fail a lot. When I seek the counsel of those who are better believers than I am, they do not understand my troubles—as though they had been *born* saints, seemingly knowing nothing of the anguish of defeat." This only confirms the observation that people without experience are not able to sympathize with others.

Why is it that our Lord does not come down from heaven as a grown-up man? Why must He be conceived as a baby in the womb of a virgin? Why must He be nursed and carried until He gradually grows up? Why must He pass through 30-odd years of sufferings on earth? Why is He not crucified—and thus accomplish the work of redemption—three days after He is born? Oh do let us see that He has suffered all these limitations and endured all these sorrows in order that He might be sympathetic towards us.

How our Lord has verily borne the misunderstandings and persecutions of men; how, too, He has experienced the scourgings and shame and rejection by men, and finally the crucifixion. He needs to taste all the bitternesses of life so as to be touched with the feeling of man's infirmities. His more than 30 years of life on earth as man and His preaching and traveling about for three years are not only for the sake of fulfilling His task and mission but also for the reason that He might be able to sympathize with us. He must do so in order that He may be touched with our infirmities. In case any reader of these pages is brokenhearted or is experiencing any heart-wound, let him realize that our Lord at this very moment is fully aware of his sorrow and is truly feeling his feeling. He not only has the grace to save you, He also has the heart to sympathize with you. In short, He feels exactly as you feel.

Experience alone, though, is not adequate enough for sympathy. The second factor needed is love. Someone may have been ill for many years and is thus enabled to know firsthand the real distress of sickness, yet even so, he is not able to sympathize with all the sick ones in the world—although it may be quite true that he can be touched with the feelings of his own loved ones who may be ill. He has experience, but he lacks love; therefore, he is not able to be sympathetic to *all* men. The Lord shows sympathy to all men because He possesses the needed love as well as the experience. Once, as He was descending from a mountain, a leper came to Him, saying, "Lord, if thou wilt, thou canst make me clean." The Lord immediately touched him with His hand and said, "I will; be thou made clean" (Matt. 8.1–3). In His heart of love there was a place for the leper; He could feel the suffering of the leper. He therefore *touched* him with His hand. Truly, the Lord has not only experience but also love.

Having experience and love, however, are still insufficient. The third factor is a being free from everything—that is to say, a not being held down by anything prior to the occasion requiring sympathy. Oftentimes one's heart is already occupied with something, so that a person is held back from even the possibility of sympathizing with other people. A person in such a preoccupied state will undoubtedly say that if he is not able to bear his own burden, how in the world will he ever have the strength to show sympathy to the burdens and distresses of others? In the case of our Lord, however, we find that one attitude which constantly characterized His life while on earth was that He forgot His own needs completely. You may never have thought of it before, but in this connection it can truly be said that what our Lord did *not* do in a given situation was often even more marvelous and meaningful than what He in fact *did* do! For example, He was hungry, yet He did not turn stone into bread to satisfy His hunger. When His enemies came to seize Him, He did not ask the Father to send twelve legions of angels to protect Him. Never was His heart occupied with His own affairs. He was never held back from sympathizing with men because He was engrossed in His own things. With us, however, frequently we are so oppressed by our own burdens that we have to pass over other people's sufferings even though we do see them. Not so in the case of our Lord. Had He only regarded the anticipated sufferings of the cross, He would have been so seized daily by His own sufferings as to leave no room to sympathize with others. For how could He have ever borne the burdens of others by helping them if He had all the time been thinking of how tremendously great and unbearable His own sufferings were? But instead, our Lord spent His days as though He had no burden to bear at all. He healed the sick and preached the gospel to the poor whenever He met them. It appeared as if He had nothing else to do. He was in full sympathy with men. Each time He went out to them His heart was like a white sheet that was ready to be impressed with the mark of any ink or image of other men's suffering. Praise and thanks be to the Lord, because His heart is always vacant—ready to be occupied by the needs of others.

He was not only sympathetic to the people of His own time; He is full of the same sympathy towards us all today. For He has now become our High Priest in heaven, always merciful to us. The hardships He endured during his lifetime on earth were tens of thousands of times more than all we can experience. Hence we can pray to Him and touch Him: "Let us therefore draw near with boldness unto the throne of grace, that we may receive mercy, and may find grace to help us in time of need" (Heb. 4.16). Whenever we have trouble He feels with us, and He will support us with grace and give us peace.

Many times you may think that nobody cares for you and that no one shows any sympathy to comfort and succour you. During such times you must feel your burdens most heavily and your heart must therefore be aching. Even so, there is One in heaven who sympathizes with you. You may come boldly to the throne of grace and ask His help. There is One who is touched with the feeling of your infirmity; and He is able to lighten your burden. Earthly friends may at times lessen your burden, but this Friend in heaven is *always* prepared to bear your heavy burden. He bears your burden not just in feeling but even more so in actuality. This High Priest sympathizes with you and gives grace to you. Though He is in heaven,

He seems to take you as His delight and He is deeply concerned with your affairs. What a Lord He is! Praise and thank God, we have such a Lord as this!

Finally, let me say that being in full sympathy with you and feeling what you feel, the Lord will give you a burden which is beyond your power to bear. Yet do remember that in each situation you find yourself in, He is with you, He feels what you feel, and He waits to dispense grace to you. Our High Priest deeply senses every difficulty of yours and understands fully each drop of your tears. He suffers as much as you suffer. Let us therefore trust Him and rest in Him. How sympathetic this High Priest is to us. And though He is not present physically today, nevertheless, His heart is always open to us. Praise His name!

TITLES YOU
WILL WANT TO HAVE

by Watchman Nee

Basic Lesson Series
Volume 1—A Living Sacrifice
Volume 2—The Good Confession
Volume 3—Assembling Together
Volume 4—Not I, But Christ
Volume 5—Do All to the Glory of God
Volume 6—Love One Another

Practical Issues of This Life

Gospel Dialogue

God's Work

Ye Search the Scriptures

The Prayer Ministry of the Church

Christ the Sum of All Spiritual Things

Spiritual Knowledge

The Latent Power of the Soul

Spiritual Authority

The Ministry of God's Word

Spiritual Reality or Obsession

The Spiritual Man

The Release of the Spirit

by Stephen Kaung

The Splendor of His Ways

The Songs of Degrees
Meditations on Fifteen Psalms

ORDER FROM:

Christian Fellowship Publishers, Inc.
Box 1021
Manassas, Virginia 22110